CHARLESTON
CELEBRATION

CHARLESTON CELEBRATION

A HISTORY OF PLEASURABLE PASTIMES
FROM COLONIAL CHARLES TOWN THROUGH
THE CHARLESTON RENAISSANCE

SHELIA WATSON

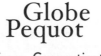

Globe
Pequot

Essex, Connecticut

Globe Pequot

An imprint of Globe Pequot, the trade division of
The Rowman & Littlefield Publishing Group, Inc.
4501 Forbes Blvd., Ste. 200
Lanham, MD 20706
www.rowman.com

Distributed by NATIONAL BOOK NETWORK

British Library Cataloguing in Publication Information available

Library of Congress Cataloging-in-Publication Data
Names: Watson, Shelia Hempton, author.
Title: Charleston celebration : a history of pleasurable pastimes from
    colonial Charles Town through the Charleston renaissance / Shelia
    Watson.
Description: Essex, Connecticut : Globe Pequot, [2023] | Includes
    bibliographical references and index. | Summary: "A journey through
    Charleston's past with a look at the talented people and inspiring
    events that shaped the city and surrounding region into a cultural mecca
    of art, music, dance, and design. Each chapter features an itinerary for
    a walking or driving tour to help readers celebrate the lesser-known
    side of Charleston's entertaining past"— Provided by publisher.
Identifiers: LCCN 2022019329 (print) | LCCN 2022019330 (ebook) | ISBN
    9781493061501 (paperback) | ISBN 9781493061518 (epub)
Subjects: LCSH: Amusements—South Carolina—Charleston—History. |
    Charleston (S.C.)—History. | Charleston (S.C.)—Tours.
Classification: LCC F279.C45 W38 2023 (print) | LCC F279.C45 (ebook) |
    DDC 975.7/915—dc23/eng/20220427
LC record available at https://lccn.loc.gov/2022019329
LC ebook record available at https://lccn.loc.gov/2022019330

CONTENTS

SECTION 2: BECOMING AMERICA   49

SECTION 3: THE BELLE OF THE BALL   85

INTRODUCTION

Many books have been written about Charleston, a fact that should surprise no one. The Grande Dame of the South has been here for centuries and has many fascinating tales to tell.

The tales are so fascinating that, I do declare, doing the research for this book was the best rabbit hole I've ever been down.

There are books and articles that detail how Charleston endured the Revolutionary War and the Civil War, write-ups that dig into specific topics like architecture or piracy, and published pieces that offer insights into the people, places, and politics.

One doesn't have to search long to find a wealth of information about Charleston: short histories, in-depth studies, surveys, compilations, the lighter side, the darker side, and a treatise on just about every aspect of the city.

This book delves into one specific aspect: Charleston's pleasurable pastimes through the years. And there are many. There's a reason Charleston keeps receiving accolades like being voted year after year as Best City to Visit, Friendliest City, Most Enjoyable Place to Visit, and so on.

The simple truth is that Charleston loves to entertain and to be entertained. She seeks out the beauty and joy and pleasure in her charming surroundings, and she invites others to enjoy them as well.

In her book, *Prints and Impressions of Charleston*, celebrated artist Elizabeth O'Neill Verner wrote that, "It is so difficult for a Charlestonian to write about Charleston without becoming either sentimental or austere."

How right she was. At one point in my research, I realized that I could either wax eloquent on every instance of entertainment—and, because the city never stops seeking enjoyment, possibly never finish the book—or accept that it might not be possible to capture and catalogue every instance of amusement throughout the years. I went with the latter, and I hope you, gentle reader, will forgive any omissions.

This book was a great pleasure for me to research and to write. It is my fervent wish that you will find great pleasure in these pages.

Shelia Watson
West of the Ashley
Charleston, South Carolina

SECTION 1: ROYAL TREATMENT

Colonial and Pre-Revolutionary Period, 1670–1773

Genteel Entertainments to All
—JOHN LAWSON, ENGLISH SURVEYOR,
FROM A DESCRIPTION OF
CHARLES TOWN IN ONE OF HIS REPORTS
WHEN THE COLONY WAS ONLY
THIRTY YEARS OLD

Timeline Highlights: 1670–1773

Elsewhere		Charleston
1672: Charles II of England issues Royal Declaration of Indulgence, promising religious freedom. 1673: Louis and Marquette explore the Mississippi River. 1675: Construction of Royal Greenwich Observatory.	1670	1670: First settlers arrive. 1672: Charles Town is reported to have thirty houses and two hundred to three hundred residents. 1676: Magnolia Plantation founded.
1680: First ballets in Germany (from France). 1681: Female dancers appear for first time at Paris opera. 1682: Louis XIV moves his court to the Palace of Versailles.	1680	1680: St. Philip's Church founded. 1681: Mepkin Plantation and Boone Hall Plantation founded. 1685: Henry Woodward receives rice, which becomes a cash crop for the area.
1692: Salem witch trials. 1698: English engineer Thomas Savery patents first steam engine.	1690	1690: Town officially moves from Albemarle Point to present location on peninsula (population twelve hundred, fifth largest city in colonies).
1700: Most countries adopt Gregorian calendar. 1704: First regular newspaper, *Boston News-Letter*, starts publishing, prints first advertisement. 1705: His Majesty's Theatre opens in London. 1705: Handel's first opera, *Almira*. 1707: Acts of Union between England and Scotland create Great Britain.	1700	1700: Town establishes tax-supported public library, first in America. 1705: Shepheard's Tavern built at corner of Broad and Church Streets.

Elsewhere		Charleston
1710: Law of Copyright established in Great Britain. 1711: Queen Anne establishes Ascot races. 1711: Alexander Pope's "Essay on Criticism" published anonymously. 1712: Slave revolt on Broadway in New York. 1712: Jonathan Swift writes "A Proposal for Correcting the English Language." 1713: Vivaldi's first opera, *Ottone in villa* opens in Venice. 1713: Scriblerus Club founded in London by Swift, Pope, Congreve, et al. 1715: Vaudevilles, popular music comedies, appear in Paris. 1715: First Waterman's race held on Thames. 1717: *The Loves of Mars and Venus*, first ballet performed in England.	1710	1712: Carolina divided into North and South, each with its own governor. 1715–1717: Yamassee War (south of Charleston) between Native Americans and British colonists. 1717: Town begins removing fortifications to allow for expansion. 1718: Blackbeard blockades Charleston. 1718: Stede Bonnet hanged.
1720: First yacht club established at Cork Harbor, Ireland. 1723: Benjamin Franklin arrives in Philadelphia at age seventeen. 1724: J. S. Bach premieres *St. John Passion*. 1724: Longman's, oldest publishing house in England still in existence, founded.	1720	1720s: Rice industry develops, becomes area's major export, brings wealth to area planters. 1720: Charleston becomes a crown colony (until 1773). 1728: Regular passenger travel and shipping begins between Charles Town and New York. 1729: St. Andrew's Society founded.

Elsewhere		Charleston
1726: Jonathan Swift publishes *Gulliver's Travels*. 1729: J. S. Bach premieres *St. Matthew Passion*.		
1731: Franklin founds a subscription library in Philadelphia. 1732: Royal Opera House opens in London. 1732: Franklin's *Poor Richard's Almanack* begins publication. 1732: Ninepins played for first time in New York. 1737: First public admittance to the Salon de Paris art exhibition at the Louvre. 1737: Licensing Act restricts number of plays in London.	1730	1732: First concert in the colonies by John Salter, organist at St. Philip's. 1734: First horse race in America; South Carolina Jockey Club founded. 1735: First opera in colonies performed. 1736: Dock Street Theatre opens. 1737: South Carolina Society founded.
1741: Handel composes *The Messiah* oratorio. 1741: Franklin founds *The General Magazine*. 1742: Handel's *Messiah* first performed in Dublin. 1745: The quadrille becomes popular dance in France. 1746: Battle of Culloden, Scotland. 1748: Court of King's Bench in England rules that "cricket is a legal sport."	1740	1740: Great Fire of 1740. 1740: Construction of East Bay warehouse district (today's Rainbow Row). 1745: Lots laid out for Ansonborough neighborhood, first suburb. 1748: Charleston Library Society organized.

Elsewhere		Charleston
1750: First playhouse opens in New York. 1751: "War of the Operas" divides Paris into pro-Italian and pro-French music lovers. 1751: First public cricket match, reported in *New York Gazette*. 1750: English Jockey Club founded in London. 1752: Franklin tests lightning conductor. 1752: Liberty Bell arrives in Philadelphia. 1753: English Jockey Club establishes permanent racetrack at Newmarket. 1754: St. Andrew's Royal and Ancient Golf Club founded in Scotland. 1755: Samuel Johnson's *Dictionary of the English Language* published in London. 1759: Voltaire's *Candide* is published in five countries to scandalous acclaim.	1750	1751: City divided into two parishes: St. Michael's south of Broad and St. Philip's north of Broad. 1752: Great Hurricane of 1752.
1760: Royal Society of Arts opens in London. 1762: Petit Trianon built by Louis XV. 1764: The Literary Club founded in London. 1764: Literary salons founded in Paris.	1760	1766: St. Cecilia Society formed. 1767: Old Exchange Building built on ruins of Half Moon Battery.

Elsewhere		Charleston
1764: At age eight, Mozart writes his first symphony. 1765: Great Britain passes Quartering Act, requiring American colonies to house British troops, and the Stamp Act, to pay for housing the troops. 1766: Parliament repeals the Stamp Act. 1767: Mozart, age eleven, writes first opera. 1768: Philip Astley stages first modern circus in London.		
1770: "Boston Massacre," brawl between civilians and British troops. 1770: Parliament repeals duties on paper, glass, and dyes, but retains duty on tea. 1770: First public restaurant opens in Paris. 1773: Boston Tea Party, protesting duty on tea. 1773: The waltz becomes popular in Vienna. 1773: Philadelphia Museum founded.	1770– 1773	1773: Charleston Library Society founds Charleston Museum, first public museum in the country. 1773: Charleston has her own tea party (thirteen days before Boston); the tea is not dumped but rather secretly stored in the Exchange Building. 1773: First Chamber of Commerce meeting.

FIRST STEP TO A LIFE OF LEISURE: BECOMING THE IDLE RICH

The Town has very regular and fair Streets, in which are good Buildings of Brick and Wood. . . . This Colony was at first planted by a genteel Sort of People that were well acquainted with Trade, and had either Money or Parts to make good Use of the Advantages that offer'd, as most of them have done by raising themselves to great Estates . . . and . . . considerable Fortunes. . . . They have a considerable Trade both to Europe and the West Indies, whereby they become rich and are supply'd with all Things necessary for Trade and genteel Living.

—JOHN LAWSON, EXPLORER, PLANT COLLECTOR, SURVEYOR, AND AUTHOR OF *A NEW VOYAGE TO CAROLINA.*

Yearning for leisure activities and having the means for leisure are two different things.

Fortunately for those in the area, the climate of Charles Town was perfect for rice and indigo. These two crops brought wealth and success to the landowners, which in turn enabled them to build churches, theaters, an exchange, a college, and other establishments that would encourage newcomers and sustain population growth.

"Carolina Gold" Rice

If rice was responsible for the area's rise to prominence in the colonial era, then Henry Woodward gets credit for bringing the crop to the colony.

Woodward is generally considered the "first South Carolinian." In 1666, four years before Charles Town was founded, he joined Robert Sandford's expedition to

Bennett Rice Mill and West Point Rice Mill *Library of Congress*

explore the region for the lords proprietors. They landed at Port Royal, and when Sandford left, Woodward stayed behind with the American Indian tribes on St. Helena Island (near present-day Beaufort).

Not much is known about Woodward's early years. He was apparently well educated and was able to learn the American Indian languages and customs, which were invaluable to the colony's first years.

In 1685 Woodward met John Thurbur, the captain of a New England sailing vessel that came to Charles Town for refitting. As thanks for Woodward's generosity during his stay, Captain Thurbur gave him a bag of Madagascar rice seed, which Woodward distributed to various landowners. After some experimentation, it grew successfully and became the "Carolina Gold" rice that brought vast wealth to the planters.

Most scholars agree that the first rice crops were produced "dry" (i.e., without irrigation and on relatively high ground), which yielded little. By the 1720s cultivation was moved from high ground to the freshwater swamps, and a systematic water-controlled process was introduced. A complete rice industry had begun.

Production improved again in the 1750s, when the crop was moved to drained swamps on or near the area's tidal rivers. Tidal cultivation allowed the daily tides to bring water on and off the fields, which irrigated the crop while reducing labor needs. In time, rice planters found the perfect locations where the tides were strong enough to raise and lower water without being too salty or brackish. These tidal rivers included the Waccamaw, Santee, Cooper, Ashley, Combahee, and Savannah.

Henry Woodward's Excellent Adventure

The story of Henry Woodward's life reads alternately like an adventure tale and a romance novel.

Born in England in 1646, he arrived in Barbados in 1665—at age nineteen already well educated and apparently with enough medical training to call himself "doctor."

He signed on as ship's surgeon with Robert Sandford's 1665 expedition to explore the lower Carolina coast, in the area that would become South Carolina. The expedition's first stop was at a small English colony on the Cape Fear River. They stayed long enough for Woodward to fall in love and marry Elizabeth Yeardley, and their union resulted in a son named Francis.

However, the expedition moved on in June 1666, and Woodward left Elizabeth behind. They explored the coast between what is now Charleston and Beaufort, before meeting with the Escamacu on St. Helena Island. The tribe was friendly, so an exchange was proposed: An Englishman would stay and learn the language and customs, and a member of the tribe would join Sandford's expedition. Woodward volunteered.

Sandford later wrote that Woodward was "treated with the greatest love and courtesy." One of the first things the Escamacu gave Woodward was the sister of the American Indian who had joined the Sandford expedition. This woman—wife number two, apparently—was given instructions to "tend him and dresse his victualls and be careful of him so her Brother might be the better used amongst us."

Woodward was supposed to stay with the Escamacu until Sandford returned; however, six months later he ended up with the Spaniards in St. Augustine—either captured or spying (the tale varies). About this time, the privateer-turned-pirate, Captain Robert Searle, attacked St. Augustine, and Woodward left with him.

After sailing for a few years with Searle and other privateers in the Caribbean, he decided to return to London. He boarded a ship in August 1669—only to be shipwrecked in a hurricane and washed ashore on the island of Nevis.

Soon an English ship stopped at the island to retrieve fresh water. It was the Carolina, one of the "first fleet" bringing the original colonists to South Carolina. Woodward came aboard and ended up back on Carolina soil.

His knowledge of Indigenous languages and cultures was instrumental in getting Charles Town established. He also helped start the lucrative American Indian trade for skins and furs.

In 1671, Woodward traveled to North Carolina and Virginia on foot and reunited with Elizabeth. Unfortunately, she thought he was dead and had remarried. He returned to Charles Town and, in payment for his "industry and hazard," he was made a lords proprietor's deputy and given two thousand acres of land.

At this point, he met wife number three: Margaret Midwinter, an indentured servant to colonist Original Jackson. Woodward had to purchase Margaret's freedom before marrying her. He canceled debts Jackson owed him for professional services, and with the "further consideration of a peppercorn," the two were married. It didn't last, and again, the story varies. While Woodward was building their home on Johns Island, Margaret sailed to England, at which point the boat either capsized or was captured by pirates and sunk. So ends the third marriage.

A few years later, around 1679, Woodward married again. Wife number four was Mary Godfrey Browne, the widow of Robert Browne and daughter of Colonel John

Godfrey, one of the colony's most important men. This union produced two sons and one daughter.

In 1685, he met John Thurbur, captain of a New England sailing vessel that had come to Charles Town for refitting. Thurbur gave Woodward a bag of rice seeds from Madagascar in exchange for the help Woodward gave him. This was the start of Charleston's rice industry.

Woodward died in 1687. Like the tales of his marriages, there are different stories about the exact circumstances of his death. But in all accounts, the story ends with his American Indian friends bringing his body back to Charles Town with a great deal of ceremony. It is not known for certain where he is buried. The assumption is that it was on his lands on Johns Island.

For a life that spanned only forty years, Woodward accomplished an incredible amount and left a legacy of famous South Carolinians as his descendants: three governors, a dozen congressmen, some of the state's most famous generals, and several clergymen, including a bishop or two.

Indigo: The Cash Crop

Indigo, a plant that produces blue dye, was grown as a trial in South Carolina during the 1670s. Unfortunately, the dyes produced in the West Indies were a better quality, and the colony could not compete.

In the 1730s, Eliza Lucas Pinckney and Andrew Deveaux experimented with cultivation and were instrumental in reintroducing the plant in the 1740s, with new cultivation techniques that produced a product equal or superior to any grown in other parts of the world.

Within a few years, the indigo industry had grown commercially and became a valuable export, second only to rice. Carolina indigo was England's primary source of blue dye in the late-colonial era.

The crop's success was due in part to successful promotion from Eliza's husband, Charles, who printed articles in the *South Carolina Gazette* promoting indigo. Equally successful were lobbying efforts on the part of London colonial agent James Crokatt, who in 1749 persuaded Parliament to subsidize Carolina indigo production by placing a bounty of six pence per pound on the dye.

Their efforts appear to have worked. In 1747, 138,300 pounds of dye (worth £16,803 sterling) were exported to England. Over the years, the amount and value of indigo exports increased, peaking in 1775 with a total of 1,122,200 pounds (valued at £242,395 sterling). England received almost the entire crop of Carolina indigo exports, though a small amount was shipped to the northern colonies.

In addition to these economic plans, the success of indigo production was due to another important factor: It worked well within the existing agricultural economy. Indigo could be grown on land that was not suitable for rice, which meant landowners and planters did not have to reconfigure their land and labor to include indigo in their crops.

NEVER TOO YOUNG TO CHANGE THE FORTUNES OF A NEW NATION

Elizabeth (Eliza) Lucas Pinckney is a prime example of how determination can be a girl's best friend.

She was born in 1722 to British army lieutenant colonel George Lucas and his wife Ann on the island of Antigua, British West Indies. Three more children would complete the family over the next few years.

At the time, girls rarely received an education beyond reading, writing, arithmetic, and social graces, but in Eliza's case those were only the beginning. Lucas sent his daughter and her inquisitive mind to a boarding school in England, where she received a formal education, including French, music, and the subject that sparked her passion: botany.

In 1738, when Eliza was sixteen, Lucas moved his family to the Carolina colony over concerns around growing political tensions between England and Spain on Antigua. Additionally, Eliza's mother was ill, and her father thought the Carolina climate would be good for her health.

The family arrived in Charles Town, where Lucas had inherited three plantations: Wappoo Plantation, a three-hundred-acre tract on the north bank of Wappoo Creek, just across the Ashley River from Charles Town; Garden Hill, a fifteen-hundred-acre timber plantation in the Ace Basin, south of Charles Town; and Waccamaw, a three-thousand-acre rice plantation in the Santee River basin, north of Charles Town.

The family settled at Wappoo Plantation, and Eliza's education became more practical and hands-on, an experience in learning the rhythm of the tidal creeks, wildlife, and land of the Lowcountry.

Eliza became familiar with the social life of her new home as well. Her neighbors, Charles Pinckney and his wife Elizabeth, introduced her to Charles Town society, and the two families became friends.

The Pinckneys were a good family to know. Charles Pinckney, South Carolina's first native-born attorney, had studied law in England and was politically active in the colony. He served as advocate general of the Court of Vice Admiralty, justice of the peace for Berkeley County, and attorney general. He was elected to the Commons House of Assembly and was a member of the Royal Provincial Council.

A year after the move, Eliza's life changed dramatically when her father was recalled to Antigua and shortly afterward her mother died.

These events left Eliza as sole manager of Wappoo Plantation and the supervisor of the overseers at the other two Lucas properties. As she took up the tasks, her father recommended that she seek the help and advice of their friend Charles Pinckney.

Pinckney visited often and provided moral support to the young girl, and Eliza developed a close friendship with Charles's wife.

But money was still short, and the Lucas properties were in disarray. Eliza mortgaged the plantations against future earnings and sought ways to improve the family fortunes, which left little time for a social life. Though Lucas tried to find a suitable husband for his daughter, in part to provide financial relief for her, Eliza rejected the idea of an arranged marriage and focused all her energy on growing crops and saving her lands.

Rejecting suitors, especially those hand-picked by her father, was an unusual action for those times. Most young girls would have accepted a marriage that was arranged like a business deal to gain wealth or property. But Eliza was not like most girls. She had other concerns—and she confided them to family friend Charles Pinckney.

After she wrote to him about the struggles with the properties, Eliza's father sent her indigo seeds from Antigua, hoping she could find a way to meet the growing demand for indigo dye in England's textile industry.

Her first attempts were not encouraging, but within three years, she had proven that indigo could be grown and processed successfully in the Carolinas.

Meanwhile, Eliza's friendship with Charles Pinckney continued to flourish. When his wife Elizabeth's health began to fail, she recommended that Charles consider marrying Eliza. After Elizabeth's death, Charles and Eliza married a few months later, with blessings from extended family.

All the while, she continued to cultivate and process indigo, and she shared her methods with her neighbors to increase English interest in Carolina indigo trade. By 1747, 134,000 pounds of indigo were shipped to England, which generated a fortune for Eliza and her neighbors.

Before the American Revolution, indigo accounted for one-third of the trade between the colonies and England—which made Charles Town the wealthiest city in the colonies.

Charles and Eliza had four children, three of whom would survive to adulthood: Charles Cotesworth Pinckney, who later was a signer of the Constitution and two-time candidate for president of the United States; Thomas Pinckney, who became a minister to Spain and a candidate for vice president; and Harriott Pinckney, who would marry Daniel Huger Horry, Jr., and live at Hampton Plantation, north of Charles Town.

In 1753, the family moved to London for five years. Soon after their return to Charles Town, Charles Pinckney contracted malaria and died. After his death, Eliza became more involved in politics and supported the Revolution with enthusiasm.

She spent time with her daughter at Hampton Plantation, where she met Francis Marion, the "Swamp Fox" himself, and helped him evade British troops by entertaining a group of them at Hampton. Eliza was also known to George Washington as the mother of two of his most devoted supporters. He made a stop at Hampton Plantation during his 1791 visit to South Carolina specifically to meet her.

In 1793, Eliza traveled to Philadelphia for breast cancer treatment. She died soon after and was buried there. George Washington was one of her pallbearers.

> *The people in general hospitable and honest, and the better sort add to these a polite gentile behaviour . . . 4 months in the year is extremely disagreeable, excessive hot, much thunder and lightning, and muskatoes and sand flies in abundance. Charles Town, the Metropolis, is a neat pretty place. The inhabitants polite and live in a very gentile manner; the streets and houses regularly built; the ladies and gentlemen gay in their dress.*
>
> —*Eliza Lucas Pinckney writing to her brother Thomas in England in 1742*

Poem by Captain Martin, captain of a British warship, a Man of War.

Charles-town 1769.
Black and white all mix'd together,
Inconstant, strange, unhealthful weather
Burning heat and chilling cold
Dangerous both to young and old
Boisterous winds and heavy rains
Fevers and rheumatic pains
Agues plenty without doubt
Sores, boils, the prickling heat and gout
Musquitos on the skin make blotches
Centipedes and large cock-roaches
Frightful creatures in the waters
Porpoises, sharks and alligators
Houses built on barren land
No lamps or lights, but streets of sand
Pleasant walks, if you can find 'em
Scandalous tongues, if any mind 'em
The markets dear and little money
Large potatoes, sweet as honey
Water bad, past all drinking
Men and women without thinking
Every thing at a high price
But rum, hominy and rice
Many a widow not unwilling
Many a beau not worth a shilling
Many a bargain, if you strike it,
This is Charles-town, how do you like it.

THEATER AND MUSIC

During the period when the colony was being founded, settled, and divided—and especially during its time as a Crown Colony (1720–1773, after the Crown bought out the original settlers, took over ownership of the Carolinas, and separated North and South Carolina)—it was a busy time, and there was plenty of work to do. But that didn't stop people from finding and creating enjoyable diversions. The early residents were prolific in that regard, with the creation of libraries, theaters, museums, and musical societies.

From the beginning, the colony's showcase of performing arts, in particular music and theater, sealed Charles Town's reputation as a place that loved to be entertained.

Essentially, if you put a stage in front of them, they'd watch and listen with rapt attention.

The individual, venues, organizations, and performances that introduced the first performing arts in the colonies during this time include the following.

Shepheard's Tavern

This establishment, built in 1705 on the corner of Broad and Church Streets, had a long room on the Church Street side, which, prior to 1751, was rented to the government for court meetings and known throughout the town as the "courtroom."

Shepheard's Tavern was one of the town's venues for banquets honoring the arrival of royal governors, and the long room was used for a variety of entertainments, including several balls that Henry Holt gave there between 1734 and 1737 as well as a pantomime ballet—*The Adventures of Harlequin and Scaramouch*, with *The Burgomaster Trick'd*, the first ballet performed in the country—that Holt and his company of dancers performed in February 1735. Holt was influential in the Charleston theater scene, having been a student of John Essex, a prominent teacher in London theaters, and an authority on French dance. While in Charles Town, he taught dance and organized several balls for the town.

The first opera in the colonies was a ballad opera entitled *Flora: or Hob in the Well*, performed at Shepheard's Tavern, February 8, 1735.

On January 11, 1735, the *South Carolina Gazette* announced that Thomas Otway's tragedy, *The Orphan, or the Unhappy Marriage*, would be attempted in the room later that month. (It was actually performed on February 18, 1735.) This posting was the first record of a theatrical season in the colonies.

The Dock Street Theatre

The Dock Street Theatre, built on the corner of Church Street and Dock Street (later renamed Queen Street), was the first building in America constructed specifically for theatrical performances. It opened on February 12, 1736, with a performance of *The Recruiting Officer*. The community gave a warm reception of the performance, and it was followed soon by a staging of the opera *Flora* that had played earlier at Shepheard's Tavern.

After the Dock Street Theatre burned in the Great Fire of 1740, a few other playhouses sprang up, including the New Theatre, built in 1754, and Church Street Theater, built in 1773.

The Dock Street Theatre was rebuilt as a hotel in the 1800s and later renovated to become a theater yet again. (See more on the Dock Street Theatre in Section 3: The Belle of the Ball and Section 5: Doing the Charleston.)

The Dock Street Theatre then and now *Library of Congress; Point North Images*

Organists, Concerts, and the St. Cecilia Society

Around 1728, St. Philip's Episcopal Church (founded in 1680 and, at that time, Anglican) imported an organ from England. Four years later, John Salter was hired as organist. He had previously taught music at a boarding school for girls that was run by his wife. This vocation earned him the distinction of being the first secular music teacher in the country. He earned another accolade when he presented the first concert in the colonies on April 19, 1732.

Following Salter as organist at St. Philip's was Charles Theodore Pachelbel. Son of the famous German organist and composer Johann Pachelbel (composer of *Canon in D*), he left Germany and arrived in Boston in 1732. From there he traveled to Trinity Church in Newport, Rhode Island, to install an organ and stayed on as organist for three years.

Eventually he made his way to Charles Town, where he organized a concert of vocal and instrumental music to celebrate St. Cecilia, patroness of musicians.

In February 1740, he began an appointment as organist at St. Philip's and remained there until his death in 1750. One of the first European composers to immigrate to the New World, Pachelbel brought with him the great Germanic organ traditions of the early eighteenth century.

By 1766, the musical celebrations had transformed into the St. Cecilia Society, a private subscription concert organization and the earliest musical society in the colonies. As a private group, it signified the ultimate "insider status" in the region. Established to provide musical entertainment, the society held an annual ball on November 22, which was the premier social event in South Carolina.

The society was modeled on concert organizations in England, and for decades it held a series of private concerts and balls, held every two weeks, with a season lasting from autumn until early spring.

Music at the concerts was performed by both amateurs and hired professionals. The repertory included orchestral, chamber, and vocal works by European masters. The society did not own its own performance space; instead, it used different venues around town, from tavern long rooms to the South Carolina Statehouse.

Since the early 1880s, its events have been held at Hibernian Hall.

Hibernian Hall exterior and interior *Library of Congress; Point North Images*

INTELLECTUAL PURSUITS AND VISUAL ARTS

O n December 28, 1748, nineteen young gentlemen of Charles Town gathered to discuss a private subscription library to support education and the arts and sciences.

Initially they kept the library's materials in their homes. But by 1755, they had secured a charter of incorporation for the Charles Town Library Society—the third-oldest institutional library in the country—and established a tradition in which the colony's royal governors were presidents of the Library Society—a tradition that lasted until the Revolutionary War.

The materials were transferred to the Free School on Broad Street, where the elected librarian was headmaster, and in 1765, the books were stored in the upstairs of a liquor warehouse owned by a prominent member. At that point, the society's book and periodical collection numbered about five thousand volumes. A few years later, the collection was transferred to the upper floor of what was then the State-house (currently the County Courthouse at Broad and Meeting).

In 1770, the society members promoted a colonial college that later became the College of Charleston, the first municipal college in the country.

Three years later, in 1773, the society started a natural science collection that became the Charleston Museum.

Henrietta de Beaulieu Dering Johnston Paints the Town

As the town settled, people flocked to enjoy the amenities. Among them were Henrietta Dering Johnston, the first professional female artist in the colonies, who completed many portraits of famous individuals.

The date and place of her birth are unknown, though the place is assumed to be northern France. Her parents were Francis and Susanna de Beaulieu, Huguenots who immigrated to London in 1687. In 1694 she married Robert Dering, the fifth son of Sir Edward Dering, and they settled in Ireland. Her husband died a few years later, leaving her a widow with two daughters.

The Charleston Museum *Library of Congress*

College of Charleston *Library of Congress*

To provide for her daughters, Henrietta painted pastel portraits on paper, a medium that had not yet gained widespread acceptance, and she signed and dated the wooden backings of the portraits. Her subjects were mostly members of her husband's extended family, which included such noted individuals as the Earl of Barrymore and Sir John Percival (later the Earl of Egmont).

In 1705 she married the Reverend Gideon Johnston, a graduate of Trinity College, Dublin, who was the vicar at Castlemore. Three years later, he was appointed bishop's commissary in South Carolina by the bishop of London, and they set off for Charles Town, where Reverend Johnston became the rector of St. Philip's Episcopal Church.

Unfortunately, all was not well in the colony. Reverend Johnston wrote many times to the Society of the Propagation of the Gospel in Foreign Parts regarding payment of his salary, which was often delayed. In one letter he noted, "Were it not for the Assistance my wife gives me by drawing of Pictures . . . I shou'd not have been able to live," which assumed that Henrietta Johnston was being paid for her portraits, thus making her the first professional woman artist in America.

Her subjects were among her circle of associates, including numerous Huguenots (the Prioleaus, Bacots, DuBoses) and various members of her husband's congregation, including Colonel William Rhett.

Today, her pastels are in private collections in Ireland and in American museums, including the Gibbes Museum of Art, the Museum of Early Southern Decorative Arts, the Metropolitan Museum of Art, and the Greenville County Museum of Art.

A LEISURELY WAY TO
DO BUSINESS

Cards, dice, the bottle and horses engross prodigious portions of time and attention.
—JOSIAH QUINCY, YANKEE PURITAN, UPON HIS VISIT TO CHARLES TOWN, 1773

Throughout all thirteen colonies, taverns were the center of social and civic life, and Charles Town was no exception.

In the years leading up to the Revolution, taverns and inns were a fundamental part of the community, though taverns were more plentiful. (In the early days, the establishment was called an "ordinary"; by the end of the seventeenth century, the word *tavern* was used.) The main difference between taverns and inns was that inns offered accommodations, whereas taverns provided only food and drink.

The taverns also served a variety of purposes, with patrons staging shows and conducting business. The local governments held public meetings, held court, and set up post offices.

The taverns in Charles Town were modeled after the coffeehouses of England after the 1660 Restoration of the Monarchy, which included a strong revival of trade and investment. Financial speculators wanted to invest in England's growing global trade, but the use of permanent formal offices was not yet standard practice. The ale houses and taverns were unsuitable, with a clientele that was often unruly. In a classic necessity-mothers-invention moment, coffeehouses began to spring up around parts of London, ready to cater to more affluent customers. There, businessmen could meet for conversation and dealing in a more refined setting.

The spaces designated for business often included meeting rooms, semi-private booths, a variety of newspapers, and a table for dining. Many of the establishments also contained long rooms, meant to mimic ballrooms in homes or palaces, that could be used for assemblies, auctions, concerts, or meetings.

These taverns also played an important part in the town's philanthropic life. In these establishments, gentlemen of assorted ethnicities and affiliations met on a regular basis and formed benevolent societies to raise funds for a wide range of causes.

During the colonial period, Charles Town was home to more than one hundred taverns/coffeehouses, including Dillon's, Swallows, Gordon's, Sign of the Bacchus, City Tavern, Henry Gignilliat's, and the Georgia Coffee House. Some of the more well known include the following.

Shepheard's Tavern / Swallow's Tavern

Shepheard's Tavern, established by Charles Shepheard c. 1720 on the corner of Broad and Church Streets, included a "long room" that served as the town's first courtroom.

The *South Carolina Gazette* announced that both the nation's first theatrical play and the first opera were staged there, both in 1735. The building burned in the Great Fire of 1740, but Shepheard rebuilt at the same location using salvaged materials. He was thereafter appointed postmaster in 1743.

Some of the most powerful men in the colony met here regularly. The St. Andrew's Society and other fraternal organizations held their meetings and dinners at Shepheard's. Solomon's Lodge No. 1 of Freemasons—the first Masonic lodge in America—was organized there in 1736, as did the Scottish Rite Freemasonry in America in 1801.

Shepheard's Tavern was one of the town's venues for banquets honoring the arrival of royal governors. Ironically, Shepheard's also served as the meeting place where Christopher Gadsden sparked the flames of the American Revolution among his rebel group that became known as the Sons of Liberty.

By the time of the Revolutionary War, the establishment was known as Swallow's Tavern (see page 53).

> The importation of liquors at Charles Town in 1743 staggers the imagination—1,500 dozen empty bottles, among other items, to be used for 'six months' supply' of 1,219 hogsheads, 188 tierces, and 58 barrels of rum.
> —Carl Bridenbaugh (1903–1992), historian, in *Myths and Realities: Societies of the Colonial South* (1952)

Dillon's Tavern

This two-story brick tavern, located in the middle of town, was well known to all. In the 1730s, it had been used as a theater and a courthouse before other structures were built. Owner Robert Dillon welcomed aid societies, gentlemen needing a place to conduct business, musical concerts, and meetings of the newly formed Jockey Club. Dillon's Tavern was also the setting for many social clubs, including the Saint Andrew's Society, the Saint George's Society, and the Fellowship Society. The Charles Town Library Society met there every Wednesday, and the Sons of Liberty were regulars. Governor Bull entertained there as well.

Given its centralized location and popularity, the tavern was host to many public protests and celebrations as the colonies geared up for a break with England.

In 1765, in the course of protesting the arrival of a ship carrying stamps for the Stamp Act, some of the townspeople erected a gallows in front of Dillon's Tavern and hung three effigies. A year later, when the Stamp Act was repealed, Dillon's Tavern was the site of the celebration, which, according to the *South Carolina Gazette*, was "a very elegant entertainment" sponsored by Lieutenant Governor William Bull. Two years later, some of the town's citizens gathered to nominate a slate of candidates for the assembly, followed by a gathering at Dillon's Tavern, complete with patriotic toasts. The crowd, led by "45 of their number, carrying as many lights, marched in regular procession down King street and Broad street to Mr. Robert Dillon's tavern; where the 45 lights being placed upon the table, with 45 bowls of punch, 45 bottles of wine, and 92 glasses, they spent a few hours in new round of toasts." Five months later, the group—now called Club 45—spent another evening "in the most social and joyous manner, drinking many loyal, patriotic, and constitutional toasts." Yet again, in 1770, upon learning that English radical John Wilkes had been released from jail, Club 45 convened for celebration at Dillon's Tavern.

Poinsett Tavern, the Two-Bit Club, and the South Carolina Society

Dr. Elisha Poinsett, a French Huguenot, opened the Poinsett Tavern on Elliott Street about 1732. By 1737, business was not going well, so a few of his friends agreed to help by dropping by a few evenings a week. Given that charity was the primary reason they met, they began to contribute two bits (sixteen pence) per week into a fund that could be used to help the needy.

South Carolina Society Hall *Library of Congress*

Word of the group spread, more people joined, and it became known as the "Two-Bit Club." Eventually the group formed an association, with charity the key focus and education the main charity.

The Provincial General Assembly incorporated the Two-Bit Club as the French Society on May 1, 1751, and King George II confirmed it at the Court of St. James on December 20, 1752. The name was later changed to the South Carolina Society and included non-French members.

The society founded schools for orphans and indigent children and later organized secondary schools for boys and girls. The society built its own hall on Meeting Street, which still exists. Today the South Carolina Society is primarily a social organization, and because of the high demand for membership, only descendants of early members are admitted.

Dr. Poinsett's descendant, Joel Roberts Poinsett, one-time ambassador to Mexico, introduced the poinsettia to the United States.

> There is not one Night in the Week in which they are not engaged with some Club or other at the Tavern where they injure their Fortunes by gaming in various Ways, and impair their Health by the intemperate Use of Spirituous Liquors and keeping late Hours, or rather spending whole Nights, sometimes, in these disgraceful and ruinous Practices.
> —From the letter of a lady in Charles Town, October 5, 1769

Other Taverns and Meeting Houses

Historic maps found in Scotland and the Netherlands note that a Seafarer's Tavern was in Charles Town in 1686, which would make it the oldest liquor store in America. For three centuries, the tavern was located on the working waterfront—in fact, it still stands today at 120 East Bay Street—and it has gone by many names, including The Tavern on the Bluffs, Harris's Tavern, the Globe Tavern, Mrs. Coates Tavern by the Bay, and others.

The Pink House at 17 Chalmers Street opened as a popular local tavern in the 1750s. It has been used for a wide range of purposes, including as a brothel, a residence, an art gallery, and a lawyer's office. The building, made of Bermuda stone with a tile roof, still stands.

Pink House then and now *Library of Congress; Point North Images*

Coates Row then and now *Library of Congress; Point North Images*

The Benjamin Backhouse Tavern hosted performances at its waterfront location, though they were not as refined as those at Dillon's. Frequent guests were typically sailors, actors, party gentry, and the local Sons of Liberty. Among the offerings were backgammon and billiards (ten tables), and gambling was encouraged. After

Backhouse passed, Henry Gray became the tavern's proprietor and turned to the *South Carolina Gazette* and *Country Journal* to inform the community of the new management. Noting that the "well frequented" tavern already had a substantial clientele, he invited the "Friends and Acquaintance of Mr. Backhouse" to continue their patronage and promised that they would continue to "meet with civil treatment" as they enjoyed "good Liquor and good Cheer."

In the early 1700s, a public house/tavern named Bowling Green was located opposite the venue for the first organized horse race, run in 1734. Beside the tavern was a bowling green, which was a mowed pitch used to play the game of "lawn bowls" (similar to the Italian game of bocce). The race course isn't shown on any map, but racing historian John Beaufain Irving wrote in 1857 that it was "in the vicinity of the spot which the lower depot of the South Carolina Railroad now occupies," which places the course roughly in the area of today's John Street. (In fact, today's Charleston Music Hall and the surrounding buildings are part of the complex that housed the South Carolina Railroad in 1857.) It is not certain whether the name Bowling Green referred to the tavern or the lawn, though it's almost certain that it was among the many houses of ill repute. An advertisement in the *South Carolina Gazette* in November 1740 provides few clues: "To be let at Christmas next, the house near Mrs. Trott's pasture, where the Bowling Green was formerly kept, with a convenient pasture adjoining."

THE GREAT OUTDOORS

Several outdoor activities were founded during this time—such as golf courses and horse racing—and many of the parks and gardens were planted, an essential cultivation of future locales of leisure as well as tourist spots.

The Sporting Life

Timothy Boardman, a native of Vermont, wrote about his visit to Charles Town in the late 1700s: "I believe there is a few who now & then go to Church, but by all Observation I have been able to make I find that Horse Racing, Frolicking . . . [and] Gaming of all Kinds . . . to be the Chief Business of their Sabbaths."

He wasn't wrong.

The residents of Charles Town did have a fondness for games and sports. No sooner had they debarked when they noticed all the empty acreage just waiting to be played or raced upon.

GOLF

The origins of golf have been debated, but general consensus holds that the game predates the colonies by several centuries, as it was first mentioned in writings in the Middle Ages, and that it originated in Scotland.

What is more certain, via shipping documents, is that golf—or more specifically, golf equipment—was brought to the colonies in 1743, when David Deas received 432 balls and ninety-six clubs in the port of Charles Town from the Scottish port of Leith.

The large number of balls and clubs arriving in Charles Town suggests several players or even the formation of a club (an assumption that later proved true).

Deas was a Scottish shipping merchant who had moved to Charles Town from Leith, where the first golf club—"The Gentlemen Golfers of Leith"—was formed in 1744. Leith also had a five-hole course and had recorded rules of the game. (For context, the club and course at St. Andrews wasn't developed until 1754.)

Sixteen years later, a Charles Town merchant, Andrew Johnston, returned from a trip to Scotland in 1759 with golfing equipment for use on his plantation. When he died five years later, the inventory of his estate listed "twelve goof [golf] sticks and balls."

Though it would be a few years before a formal club was established, at this point there were enough pieces of equipment to gather a group and play. The game was on.

HORSE RACING

In the early years, Charles Town was the seat of racing, even with its humble beginnings. The first horse race, announced in the *South Carolina Gazette*, occurred in 1734 at a temporary course near the public house/tavern named Bowling Green. The prize was a saddle and bridle worth twenty pounds.

The same year, the town formed a jockey club, the first in the country.

The first permanent track, the York Course, was built the next year near the Quarter House Inn on the Charles Town Neck (the upper peninsula) and served as the main horse racing venue until the 1750s. Races were held every year, with a silver trophy worth about 100 pounds given as a prize.

Later a new track was built on the edge of what was then downtown. Called the New Market Race Course after the famed course in England, it hosted its first race in 1760, at which time the rules of racing were established, and prizes of silver or gold were awarded in its yearly event. Its proprietor offered stables and the annual "Charles Town Races" until the Revolutionary War.

The sport was so popular that horse breeding became a new industry in the area. Horsemen from Charles Town and the inland river settlements, intent on improving the breed, began importing fine stallions and mares from England and Virginia.

The South Carolina Jockey Club predated the English Jockey Club by sixteen years. Today the English Jockey Club continues to organize English racing, and the United States eventually founded its own national-level club based on the English organization.

Gardening

Charles Town saw the first plantings of many of the iconic southern shrubberies and flora including the magnolia, gardenia, camellia, and azalea. These were planted in abundance, and across the region, homes sported gardens, often paying more attention to their upkeep than the dwellings.

The owners of the larger plantations took special care to cultivate gardens for pleasure along with their money-making crop fields. We owe those landowners a great deal of respect for their foresight and provision, especially considering some of their plans and designs would not come to fruition in their lifetimes.

MAGNOLIA PLANTATION AND GARDENS

Founded in 1676, Magnolia contains the oldest public gardens in America.

Thomas Drayton and his wife, Ann, traveled from Barbados to the Charles Town colony and established the plantation on the banks of the Ashley River.

The plantation, through the agriculture of rice on the grounds, brought tremendous wealth to the Draytons during the colonial period.

During the Revolutionary War, both British and American troops alternately occupied the grounds, though the Drayton sons both became American statesmen and fought against British rule.

Years later, in the 1840s, the founder's grandson, John Grimke Drayton, enhanced the gardens, taking a softer, less formal, more natural approach to the garden's

Woman among flowering shrubs at Magnolia Gardens, circa 1900 *Library of Congress*

planning. He planted the first azaleas (*rhododendron indica*) at Magnolia and was among the first to use Camellias (*camellia japonica*) in an outdoor setting.

MEPKIN PLANTATION

Originally known as Makkean by the Cusabo tribe, Mepkin played a part in the origins of the United States.

In 1681, three sons of Sir John Colleton, one of the lords proprietors who settled the Charles Town colony, received a Proprietary Grant for three thousand acres on the west side of the Cooper River.

In 1762, a descendent of the surviving brother sold the estate to Henry Laurens, who at that time was a merchant in Charles Town. In 1776, just before the outbreak of war, he left his business and devoted himself to developing the plantation and formal gardens.

Laurens became a devoted patriot during the war, served as a delegate to the Second Continental Congress, and succeeded John Hancock as president of the Congress. He signed the Articles of Confederation and was president of the Congress when the articles were passed in 1777. His oldest son, John Laurens, was Washington's aide-de-camp and a colonel in the Continental Army.

In 1779, Laurens was captured at sea by a British ship and taken to London, where he was imprisoned in the Tower for nearly two years—the only American ever to have been held prisoner there. He was released in exchange for General Lord Cornwallis. In 1783, he was sent to Paris as one of the negotiators for the Treaty of Paris.

He returned to Mepkin in 1784 and lived in the overseer's cottage while the main house was being rebuilt (having been burnt by the British during the war). He was asked to return to the Continental Congress, but he declined, preferring the work on his plantation to public service.

He died in 1792 and was cremated—the first formal cremation in the United States—and his ashes were interred at Mepkin.

Mepkin Plantation was later purchased by Henry and Clare Booth Luce, who made further improvements to the property and eventually bequeathed it to the Roman Catholic Church, which created a monastery called Mepkin Abbey.

BOONE HALL PLANTATION

This plantation is one of the oldest in the country that is still in operation, continually producing crops for more than 320 years.

The earliest reference is a land grant in 1681 of 470 acres from Theophilus Patey to his daughter Elizabeth and her new husband, Major John Boone, as a wedding gift.

Major Boone was one of the early settlers of the Charles Town colony, and he and his wife were direct ancestors of Founding Fathers Edward Rutledge and John Rutledge.

In 1743, Boone's son planted live oak trees, arranged in two evenly spaced rows, that later became the prototypical image of plantation scenery when the massive branches met overhead, forming a moss-laden canopy.

Boone Hall Avenue of the Oaks then and now *Library of Congress*

MIDDLETON PLACE

In the 1730s, South Carolina planter John Williams began construction of a house on a large plot of land with a tactical view of the Ashley River. After his death a few years later, the property became part of the dowry of his daughter, Mary, who married Henry Middleton in 1741.

He completed a large main house—and later added two wings that included a library, ballroom, and guest house—by the end of 1741. At that point, he turned his attention to the gardens.

Although Middleton Place had a thriving rice plantation, the grounds were developed more as a country residence than a working plantation. Determined to surpass the work of his neighbors (which included the exquisite landscaping of Mepkin and Magnolia), Middleton hired an English gardener, who laid out turf terraces with bowed centers, excavated a pair of lakes (known as the "Butterfly Lakes"), and dammed a stream to enclose the rice fields.

Middleton Place, 1938 *Library of Congress*

After his wife's death in 1761, he moved to a small house in Charles Town and gave Middleton Place to his son, Arthur.

Roughly a decade later, Arthur signed the Declaration of Independence, and during the Revolutionary War, British troops invaded the area. In the ensuing Siege of Charles Town, the British plundered Middleton Place, which included beheading many of the statues in the gardens and looting the artwork and furniture in the house. Arthur Middleton was also captured and imprisoned until 1781.

In 1783, Middleton Place was the location for the signing of surrender terms that abolished British troops from the southern colonies.

After Arthur's death in 1787, the plantation passed to his eldest son, Henry, who continued to expand and develop the gardens. He introduced the first Asiatic azalea (*rhododendron indica*) and crape myrtle (*lagerstroemia indica*) to America.

Henry also imported water buffalo from Constantinople. The water buffalo, the first in America, were used experimentally to work in the deep muck of the rice fields.

Upon his death in 1846, Middleton Place passed to Henry's son, Williams, who signed the South Carolina Order of Secession in 1860. In 1865, near the end of the war, Union troops captured Middleton Place and burned the main house. The troops killed and ate five of the water buffalo and stole six, which later ended up in the Central Park Zoo in New York.

A Passion for the Botanical

Martha Daniell Logan was born into a wealthy family in 1704. Her father was twice lieutenant governor and owned a large estate. Logan learned to take care of a home—spinning, sewing, cooking—like most girls of the time.

But she was interested in plants and seeds. Her father died when she was thirteen, so she began to cultivate plants from the nurseries on the property she inherited, some forty-eight thousand acres on the Wando River north of Charleston.

She married a year later and had eight children, whom she taught at home. When her husband died in 1764, she moved her family to town and taught at a boarding school.

She never lost her love of cultivation. While she was teaching and rearing her family, she was also writing to other gardeners and botanists, trading seeds and roots with them.

Alexander Garden, born in Scotland in 1730, was a physician and naturalist.

While studying at Marischal College in Aberdeen, he apprenticed under Dr. James Gordon, who introduced him to botanical studies and "tinctured my mind with a relish for them."

He continued to study botany while pursuing a medical degree at the University of Edinburgh and worked under Charles Alston, professor of botany and medicine, as well as keeper of the garden at Holyrood and king's botanist.

In search of a warmer climate, Garden set out for South Carolina in 1751. He purchased a townhome and a country estate, Otranto. As luck would have it, his townhome was next door to Martha Logan. Within days of his arrival in Charles Town, he began sending indigenous plants to colleagues across the Atlantic, a practice he continued over the next decade.

He lived for many years in Charles Town, pursuing horticultural experiments in the gardens of both of his homes. He discovered several new genera of plants and exchanged plants and seeds with prominent botanists and plant dealers in Europe and America. The flowering shrub gardenia was named in his honor.

During the summer of 1754, Garden visited Coldengham, the Hudson Highland estate of the Scottish physician and amateur botanist Cadwallader Colden. While there he met the Philadelphia nurseryman John Bartram, who was collecting plants in the area.

Returning to America, Garden visited Philadelphia and spent several days touring Bartram's botanic garden and nursery. He invited Bartram to Charles Town, where he met Martha Logan.

Thus began a correspondence between the three plant aficionados that lasted for several years and resulted in the propagation of many of the plants in the Charleston area.

Logan later published The Gardener's Kalendar [sic], *which became a standard for state gardeners, and contributed a gardening guide for John Tobler's* South Carolina Almanack.

She advertised her roots, cuttings, and seeds from her nursery in the South Carolina Gazette.

A SWASHBUCKLING GOOD TIME

Another notable group in Charles Town during this time were pirates. From its founding in 1670, the colony became a hot spot for these swashbucklers. At that point, the government was not well organized, which gave the pirates a perfect place to appropriate.

For the most part, the pirates were tolerated, if not indulged, to the extent of having their own boardinghouse and gambling den that also served as a place where local

The Pirate House then and now *Library of Congress; Point North Images*

merchants could trade in contraband goods. The Pirate House is still standing today at 145 Church Street.

The coveted goods (booty from captured ships) that the pirates brought to the area included rum, madeira, sugar, spices, cocoa, tobacco, cotton, wood, cloths, and more.

It was a profitable business arrangement: Merchants got bargain prices for the loot, and the pirates were big spenders.

The economic boom caused the government officials and local proprietors to look the other way when pirates came to town. Blackbeard once bragged about his popularity, saying that there was not a home in the Carolinas where he wouldn't be invited for dinner. It may have been an exaggeration, but the general sentiment was correct.

Eventually, residents started to complain that pirates were bringing a little more excitement than they wanted. Additionally, the pirate ships—which had grown to the thousands—were disrupting legitimate commerce trade in the Atlantic.

Piracy had become an annoyance to local officials, and both their business and their frolicking were no longer welcome.

Pirates of Charles Town

During the "Golden Age of Piracy," which lasted roughly from 1670 to 1720, Charles Town was visited by many of the buccaneers, but these four stand out in Charles Town's history.

BLACKBEARD

Blackbeard, also known as Edward Teach, arrived in Charles Town in May 1718 and set up a blockade of the port, taking hostage several ships that included many high-ranking residents. His ransom demand wasn't the usual booty; it was a chest full of medicine, mercury in particular. At that time, mercury was thought to be a cure for venereal diseases, which many of his crew were suffering from. After a few days in the harbor, their ransom was delivered. He and his crew took the time to get drunk in the town's taverns before returning their hostages to shore and setting sail.

STEDE BONNET

With a privileged upbringing, fancy clothes, and polished manner, Bonnet was known as the "Gentleman Pirate." (According to legend, when he bought his first ship, the *Revenge*, he outfitted it with his library.) He and his crew spent the first months of his pirate career wreaking havoc on the Carolina coastline. Before long, his mentor Blackbeard tricked him into signing control of the *Revenge* over to him. To regain control of his ship, Bonnet helped Blackbeard in his 1718 blockade of Charles Town. Whereas Blackbeard managed to get away, Bonnet was soon captured and hanged at White Point (which at the time was a popular spot for pirate executions, but today is White Point Garden beside the Charleston Battery).

CHARLES VANE

A few months after Blackbeard's blockade, Charles Vane set up off Charles Town and attacked and plundered several ships. By this time, the town was on edge and ready to be rid of all pirates. Governor Robert Johnson sent William Rhett out with two Royal Navy ships and an order to capture Vane. Although Rhett didn't capture Vane, he did manage to find Stede Bonnet and thirty-four other pirates and brought them back to Charles Town.

ANNE BONNY

Born in Ireland, Anne Cormac and her parents relocated to Charles Town. Bored with life on her father's plantation, Anne met and later married pirate James Bonny. (Legend has it her father disowned her and, in retaliation, she burned his plantation to the ground.) Anne and James fled to Nassau, where she left him and became romantically involved with another pirate, John "Calico Jack" Rackham. She joined Jack's crew, disguising herself as a man, and became known as a violent pirate and expert fighter. She eventually discovered another woman in disguise (Mary Read) on the ship, and the two became friends. When their ship was captured, all of them were sentenced to hang except Anne and Mary, as they were both pregnant. Mary died in jail a short time later, but Anne's fate was uncertain, as she disappeared from any historical records at that point. (Again, legend speaks up with the myth that Anne's father relented and brought her back to Charles Town, where she lived out the rest of her life under an assumed name.)

SEE FOR YOURSELF: COLONIAL AND PRE-REVOLUTIONARY PERIOD

When you're in town, be sure to see where history was made during the colonial and pre-Revolutionary period with these tours.

CHARLES TOWNE LANDING

1500 Old Towne Rd., Charleston, 29407

Charles Towne Landing is considered the "Birthplace of South Carolina." The park is located off the Ashley River at the point where the first settlers arrived, so there's no better place to see for yourself what the earliest days looked like.

To get to Charles Towne Landing, take a short ride from the peninsula across the Ashley River Bridge. Bear right onto SC 61, then after a few miles, bear right again onto Old Towne Road. Charles Towne Landing will be on the right.

Charles Towne Landing, one of only a handful of original settlement sites in the country, is part of the South Carolina State Park system and sits on property donated to the state by Ferdinanda Legare Waring (for more info on her, see page 174 in Section 5).

You can follow the History Trail signs, tune in to an audio guided tour, or wander around at will.

Among the features are:

- A total of 664 acres, with eighty acres of gardens
- Seven miles of trails, paved and unpaved, for walking or biking
- Picnic tables
- A museum located within the visitor center containing a twelve-room exhibit hall with interactive exhibits that detail the first ten years of the colony
- An animal forest (zoo), a twenty-two-acre natural habitat zoo, home to various species that were in the colony at the time of its founding

The Adventure at Charles Towne Landing. There, you can take a tour and explore the ship.
Point North Images

- A large wooden sculpture called *Landing Brave*, depicting the head of a Native American, carved by Peter Toth and donated to Charles Towne Landing in 1977
- A sculpture, called *The Cassique*, commemorating the Kiawah chief, created by Charleston sculptor Willard Hirsch and unveiled in 1971
- Ruins of the Horry-Lucas Plantation House and the Legare Waring House, built in the 1840s (now used for events), which is on the National Register of Historic Places
- An early settler area with a palisade wall, a replica of the "stocks" used for punishment, a historic garden with samplings of the cash crops the early settlers grew, and a common house used for meetings
- Earthen fortifications and cannons set up as they might have been in the early days
- A scenic view of the marsh, Ashley River, and beyond, the City of Charleston
- The *Adventure*, a replica of the first ships that arrived in the colony
- Burial sites and cemeteries—African-American cemetery and a Native American Ceremonial Center

Occasionally the park has archaeological digs where visitors can observe or participate. Bikes are available to rent—though they are not permitted in the animal forest—and strollers and wheelchairs are available free of charge.

Be sure to see Founders Hall—an event space located across the parking lot from the visitor center—to see the plaques commemorating Henry Woodward (for more info on him and his contribution to Charles Towne, see page 7).

Walking Tour of the City Market, the US Custom House, the Waterfront Park, Castle Pinckney

This walking tour takes you about six blocks through the market area and nearby park.

Start at the City Market Great Hall at Market and Meeting Streets.

CITY MARKET

When the city was founded in 1680 (after moving from West of the Ashley where Charles Towne Landing is now located), this market area was a deep-water creek known as Daniel's Creek.

By 1704, a wall of brick and cypress was built along the Cooper River waterfront for the city's defense. The sixty-two-acre walled city was bounded by what is now East Bay, Meeting, Cumberland, and Water Streets.

In 1788, Charles Cotesworth Pinckney—a signer of the US Constitution and son of Eliza Lucas Pinckney—donated the land around Daniel's Creek to the city to be used as a marketplace. Soon after, the area was filled in and vendor sheds were built. In 1807, the area was established as the Centre Market by city ordinance, which stated it would be open every day except Christmas Day. (This ordinance is still in effect.)

Note: Many tourists assume that slaves were sold at the City Market, which is not true. Both slaves and free Blacks sold their products in this market. Slaves were sold on the waterfront until the city banned public auctions in 1856, at which time auctions were moved to an area between Chalmers and Queen Streets, where a "Slave Mart Museum" is located today.

The Great Hall, built in 1841, is a United States National Register Landmark. Initially, the upper level contained two rooms for transacting market business and one large hall for social functions. Today it houses a museum. The lower level of the Hall contains a corridor of micro-boutiques.

The remainder of the market, which runs from Meeting Street to East Bay Street, features booths inside vendor sheds as well as shops and restaurants along North Market and South Market Streets.

When you reach the end of the market, cross East Bay Street and continue to Concord Street. The Custom House is on the right.

THE CUSTOM HOUSE

By the mid-nineteenth century, at a time when trade was increasing in the port city, the US Customs Service had outgrown its offices in the Exchange Building on East Bay Street. In 1847, Congress appropriated funds to purchase the land at what was then the site of Craven's Bastion, a colonial-era fortification.

Construction began in 1853, but with rising costs and the possibility of secession, Congress did not fund the project any further. The Civil War brought

The Custom House amid construction *Library of Congress*

work to a halt, and the partially completed building was damaged during the city's bombardment.

After the war, construction resumed with revised plans and was completed in 1879. The building has a cross plan with two facades: one facing downtown on the west, the other facing the harbor on the east.

In 1960, the Charleston Historic District, which included the US Custom House, was designated a National Historic Landmark. The building was listed individually in the National Register of Historic Places in 1974.

The steps of the building—both front and back—have been used throughout the years for political and social gatherings and for the occasional concert.

At Concord Street, turn right (the harbor-facing façade of the US Custom House will be on the right) and continue two blocks to the Waterfront Park.

WATERFRONT PARK

This ten-acre park overlooks the Cooper River and Charleston Harbor. Historically, this tract of land was the center of maritime commerce, with several wharfs and shipping terminals. The city acquired the land in the 1970s, construction began on the park in the 1980s, and it opened in May 1990.

In 2007, the Waterfront Park was awarded the Landmark Award from the American Society of Landscape Architects and the National Trust for Historic Preservation.

The park includes sunny greenspaces, shaded areas with Charleston benches, a gazebo-shaded pier with family-sized swings, and two fountains (one a play fountain and one in the shape of the iconic Charleston pineapple). At the end of the pier, you can catch a water taxi that goes to the Maritime Center (farther up the peninsula), Patriots Point, and the Harbor Marina—the latter two across the Cooper River in Mount Pleasant.

From the Waterfront Park, look out into the harbor to see Castle Pinckney.

Waterfront Park Pier *Point North Images*

CASTLE PINCKNEY

Located on Shutes Folly Island, a small island in the middle of the harbor, the original structure was built in 1804 and named Fort Pinckney after Charles Cotesworth Pinckney. The log and earthen fort was intended to protect the city against attack; however, it was destroyed by a hurricane later that year.

It was rebuilt in 1810 with brick and mortar and renamed Castle Pinckney. Over the years, it was alternately garrisoned (during the War of 1812 and the Nullification Crisis of 1832) and abandoned. By the mid-1800s, it was used as a storehouse for gunpowder and other materiel.

In the 1850s, it was garrisoned once again, joining the other strategic defenses ringing the harbor: Fort Sumter and Fort Moultrie. In 1860, after South Carolina seceded from the Union, the fort was surrendered to the Confederates, and the US Army garrison joined Major Anderson at Fort Sumter. After the First Battle of Bull Run, Castle Pinckney was used as a prisoner of war camp.

After the war, it again fell into disuse. In 1890, parts of its walls were dismantled to make way for a harbor lighthouse, which operated into the twentieth century.

Castle Pinckney was declared a US National Monument in 1924 by presidential proclamation. In 1951, Congress passed a bill to abolish it as a national monument and transferred it back to the US Army Corps of Engineers, which listed it as excess property for sale in 1956. In 1958, the South Carolina State Ports Authority acquired it as a spoil area, but such plans proved impractical. The Authority tried to return the island to the federal government, but the offer was rejected. The Authority received offers to convert the island into a private residence, a nightclub, and a restaurant, but all offers were declined.

The fort eventually reverted to state ownership, and in 1970, Castle Pinckney was listed on the National Register of Historic Places. It is not accessible, though it can be viewed more closely on harbor boat tours.

No shot was ever fired from Castle Pinckney during its existence as a military fort.

SECTION 2:
BECOMING AMERICA

Revolutionary Period, 1774–1791

*Charleston is one of the most beautiful and
well-built of cities, and its inhabitants are among the
most agreeable people I have ever seen.*
—MARQUIS DE LAFAYETTE

Timeline Highlights: 1774–1791

Elsewhere		Charleston
1774: First Continental Congress adjourns in Philadelphia.	1774–1779	1774: Charlestonians Henry Middleton, John Rutledge, Edward Rutledge, Thomas Lynch, and Christopher Gadsden are named delegates to the First Continental Congress. Henry Middleton is chosen president.
1774: Louis XVI and Marie Antoinette become king and queen of France.		
1774: Philadelphia becomes first capital of United States.		
1774: Continental Congress orders discouragement of entertainment for all colonies.		1776: Declaration of Independence read aloud at Liberty Tree (near present-day 80 Alexander Street).
1775: Second Continental Congress held; US Post Office established, Continental Army, Navy, Marine Corps established.		1777: Marquis de Lafayette arrives in Georgetown, then travels to Charleston, then to Washington's camp, where he is made major-general.
1775: George Washington appointed commander in chief of Continental Army.		
1775: First Thames Regatta.		1778: Edward McCrady acquires property on East Bay Street that will become McCrady's Tavern.
1775: Mozart's opera *The Shepherd King* first produced in Salzburg.		
1776: Declaration of Independence is adopted by Second Continental Congress.		1779: Battle of Stono Ferry (south of Charleston).
1776: First volume of Edward Gibbon's *The Decline and Fall of the Roman Empire* published.		1779: General Washington orders fourteen hundred Continentals to join forces defending Charles Town.
1777: First advertisement for ice cream in *New York Gazette*.		1779: British lay siege to Charleston for forty days.

Elsewhere		Charleston
1777: Articles of Confederation, first constitution of United States, approved by Continental Congress. 1779: Army Corps of Engineers established. 1779: First Derby established at Surrey, England. 1779: First running of The Oaks horse racing.		
1781: General Washington captures Yorktown, Virginia. British General Cornwallis surrenders. 1782: Representatives from United States and Great Britain sign Treaty of Paris. 1783: Last of Great Britain's troops leave America. American Continental Army is disbanded. 1783: American Revolutionary Group, Society of the Cincinnati (the first veterans' group) founded. 1787: The dollar is accepted as the mode of currency for the United States. 1787: US Constitution is signed in Philadelphia. 1787: Mozart's *Don Giovanni* performed in Prague.	1780	1780: Charleston falls to the British and remains occupied until 1782. 1783: City officially adopts the name Charleston. 1785: College of Charleston is chartered (founded in 1770). 1786: State capital moved from Charleston to Columbia. 1786: Golf Club founded in Charleston. 1787: Recent immigrant to Charleston Jonathan Lucas invents the rice mill.

Elsewhere		Charleston
1789: Washington is unanimously elected first president of the United States. 1789: Citizens of Paris storm the Bastille. 1789: United States Department of Treasury established with Alexander Hamilton as first treasurer.		
1790: First State of the Union address; first convening of Supreme Court; Bill of Rights becomes law; Washington, District of Columbia established as country's capital. 1790: First copyright statute in United States. 1791: First performance of Mozart's *The Magic Flute* in Vienna.	1790–1791	1791: President Washington arrives for a week-long visit. 1791: Jockey Club moves venue to its final destination, Washington Race Course.

FOOD AND DRINK

During the Revolutionary War, many of the sources of leisure and entertainment were set aside, especially when Charles Town was occupied, from May 12, 1780, to December 14, 1782. Leisure can be difficult when surrounded by an occupying army; the need to gather, however, remained.

Swallow's Tavern

During the Revolutionary period, this tavern (formerly Shepheard's Tavern, see page 24, and Mr. Holliday's Tavern) was among those that hosted meetings of the Sons of Liberty.

In 1773, the first Chamber of Commerce in America was formed on the site.

After the war, on August 29, 1783, forty-three Patriot officers gathered at the tavern and formed the South Carolina Society of the Cincinnati—the country's first veterans' association. Their mission was to preserve the principles of liberty for which its founders had fought during the Revolution and to continue those values through the ages with their descendants. Major General William Moultrie, hero of the battle of Fort Sullivan, was elected its first president.

This group is the only Southern society to have remained in continuous existence since its founding.

> On January 17, 1781, the Knights Terrible Society was organized at Mr. Holliday's Tavern for the purpose of drinking once a week during the British occupation. They disbanded after the British evacuated the city.

McCrady's Tavern

The four-story Georgian house on East Bay Street was first mentioned in a plat and deed dated June 1767. The building was acquired in August 1778 by Edward McCrady, a barber, an inventor, a horse breeder, and, with this transaction, a tavern owner. In 1779, he began offering meals and lodging and built a separate kitchen to reduce the threat of fire.

Between 1778 and 1788, McCrady purchased three separate adjacent properties, which allowed him to construct a long room behind the tavern with additional access from nearby Unity Alley. The long room was used for banquets and theatrical performances.

McCrady, a devout patriot and active member of the Revolutionary militia of Charleston, was captured during the occupation of Charleston and sent to a prison in St. Augustine along with other militia leaders. He returned to

Top: McCrady's Tavern in disarray *Photograph by Charles N. Bayless, Library of Congress*
Bottom: McCrady's Tavern's Long Room in present day *Wikimedia Commons*

Charleston in 1781, and his tavern became the hub of social activities in the years following the Revolution.

When President George Washington visited Charleston in 1791, McCrady's was one of his stops. The long room was the site of a thirty-course banquet held in Washington's honor by the Society of the Cincinnati. Present for the feast were the governor of South Carolina, lieutenant governor and civil officers of the State, the mayor and aldermen of Charleston, and members of Congress and other dignitaries in President Washington's traveling party. (See page 65 for details of the visit.)

Though there were several prominent taverns with long rooms in Charleston during and after the Revolution, McCrady's is the only surviving one. After McCrady's death in 1801, the property continued as a tavern until 1884, when it became a warehouse. In 1913 it was used as a print shop. The building was damaged by fire in the early twentieth century, and afterward the front façade was altered to its present appearance. It was listed in the National Register on September 14, 1972. It was restored as a restaurant and tavern in the early 1980s and again in 2006.

> The degree to which Charlestonians took entertainment seriously is noted in an invoice for a celebration party for the fifty-five drafters of the Constitution. The tally included: fifty-four bottles of Madeira, sixty bottles of claret, eight bottles of whiskey, twenty-two bottles of port, eight bottles of hard cider, twelve beers, and seven bowls of alcohol punch "large enough that ducks could swim in them." Members of the Charleston delegation—consisting of John Rutledge, Charles Pinckney, Pierce Butler, and Charles Cotesworth Pinckney—were in charge of refreshments.

Public Houses

After the war, public meetings of the laboring classes called for British merchants and Tories to be expelled from the city. Instead, the city legislature simply changed the name from Charles Town to Charleston and corrected the pronunciation to sound like, "CHAHLston" as a way of announcing her independence from England. Charleston's reputation as the utmost in polite society was established.

After all, there were more important things to think about besides showing enemies the town limits—like eating, drinking, and making merry.

Public houses were known by various names—coffeehouse, long room, tavern, inn, hotel—and sometimes the individual establishment combined more than one type to suit the new forms of dining, drinking, and socializing.

Though most had been around for some time, by the postwar years, they were becoming more established. The exception was the hotel, which developed in the 1790s around the same time restaurants became customary. Most hotels offered grander lodgings than inns provided, along with more elaborate dining and bars.

After the war, despite the lack of stable currency and disrupted trade in oil, wine, and other staples of fine dining, Charleston strove to recapture her reputation as the epitome of fine entertainment, which was accomplished by offering the utmost in hospitality to merchants and visitors.

Thus began a rivalry among various establishments on the peninsula, which eventually produced the high standards for fine dining for which Charleston is known, even today.

In the spring of 1783, Mrs. Ramadge, proprietor of the Coffee House on the corner of Broad and Church Streets, was the first to combine the amenities of a coffeehouse with the cheerfulness of a tavern when she installed a bar among her coffee urns.

A month later, William Thompson, a gentleman from Pennsylvania, opened the City Tavern at 92 Broad Street. Though he had no room for lodgers, he advertised the quality and variety of his food and drink. He noted that his tavern included a "Coffee-room, for the benefit of Merchants and other persons, together with the Newspapers of the day, as in the best kept Coffee-Houses of this Continent." He also had a long room that he rented out for assemblies and club gatherings.

Sampson Clark, who ran the Exchange Coffee House on the corner of Broad and East Bay Streets, across from the Charleston Exchange, highlighted not only the quality of his food, but also his London-based cook named Jones. He advertised "dinners, suppers, &c. when bespoke, on the shortest notice, and elegantly dressed, in the English and French taste." One of the delicacies featured at the Exchange Coffee House was Green Turtle Soup, offered every Monday, Wednesday, and Friday. The large turtles were caught in the Caribbean and transported live to ports in North America, and the dish came to define quality dining along the East Coast. Later mock turtle soup and oyster stew were on the menu as well.

Not to be outdone, pastry chef and confectioner Augustine Moore opened a shop at 20 Meeting Street that offered the same soups and other meals offered by the Exchange Coffee House, as well as a wide variety of iced cakes, custards, jellies, and pastries.

In December 1785 he bought the Exchange Coffee House, effectively becoming the premier culinary master in Charleston. In the announcement of the ownership change, it was pointed out that chocolate, tea, and coffee were available between 8:00 a.m. and 8:00 p.m., and soups were available at 11:00 a.m.

At this point, fine dining had taken shape in post-Revolutionary Charleston. Thereafter, a public host or hostess dare not neglect food.

At the Exchange Coffee House, besides beef steak (the signature dish of Great Britain), Moore advertised ham and veal as everyday offerings. When William Robeson owned the property, he advertised a list of main dishes that included "Oysters, dressed in every desirable manner, and all kinds of Poultry, roasted and boiled, hot and cold; with Relishes, to be had all hours in the day." Oysters were served raw on the shell, stewed, roasted, and pickled.

In 1785, Mrs. Fishers on Unity Alley was considered the best in oyster suppers and pickled oysters.

Other venues through the 1780s and 1790s advertised turkeys, ducks, chickens, and guinea fowls, along with fish and game.

Around these major venues were a variety of public places where alcohol was served, with or without food. In 1783, ninety-three premises were licensed to sell alcohol, including grocery stores, boardinghouses, brew houses, dram shops, and taverns. Thirty-four of the licensees were women.

Sally Seymour Caters to the City of Charleston

Sally Seymour, the slave mistress of planter Thomas Martin and mother of his children, became a renowned caterer and culinary teacher.

In the late 1780s, as she managed Martin's house and kitchen, she learned Parisian culinary art from Adam Prior, one of Charleston's two pastry cooks. Eventually, she surpassed his skills and became more sought after than her teacher.

She also trained a generation of African-American men and women in the art of pastry cooking, which accounts for the traditional Charleston vegetables being cooked in the French style with balanced flavor in the dishes.

Many of the planters had their kitchen slaves trained by Seymour in a quasi-apprenticeship. Those she taught were in great demand as "complete pastry cooks."

Martin emancipated her in 1795 and, as a free woman of color, she set up a cook shop at 78 Tradd Street, where for almost thirty years, she was considered the best culinary artist in the city.

It was at this venue that Thomas Grimké, General Charles Cotesworth Pinckney, and General Thomas Pinckney convened the Mutton Chop Club, where every other Wednesday, they dined and talked Federalist politics and rice planting.

SPORTS CLUBS

Strained relations with the mother country and impending war didn't stop the residents of Charleston from enjoying leisure activities, especially the sports they loved. Golf and horse racing had already made their way to the area; now it was time to get serious about forming clubs and creating rules.

Golf

In 1786, Scottish merchants in Charleston formed the first golf club in the United States. Known as "Harleston Green," it was a piece of undeveloped pasture on the peninsula used as a public park, located between Calhoun and Beaufain Streets and from Rutledge Avenue to what was then the border of the Ashley River (and what is today Barre Street).

The club's launch was likely more a social event than a competitive sport. An advertisement in the *South Carolina Gazette* in 1788 asks club members to "meet at Harleston Green (and) to adjourn at William's coffee house."

The early golf games were rudimentary at best. They were played without designated tee areas and without a set number of holes. Instead, they used holes they dug into the ground, and the holes weren't marked, so they had "finders" stand next to the hole to mark it. To alert other players about an approaching shot, they yelled, "Be forewarned!" which eventually was shortened to "Fore!"

The ball was made from bull-hide and boiled goose feathers and was known as a "feathery." They typically lasted about two rounds. The clubs were made of wood and looked more like today's hockey sticks.

The club in Charleston also instituted membership fees that were used to "maintain the green"—the official origin of green fees.

Despite the humble beginnings, the game proved popular among the townsfolk, especially the Scottish shipping merchants. In time, the game and the club became more refined—and more closely resembling the Royal and Ancient Golf Club in St. Andrews, Scotland. By 1795, newspapers referred to a Harleston Green Club House.

Horse Racing

Horse racing continued in earnest into the 1770s, with Race Week the most important time of the year for residents throughout the state.

When disagreements with the mother country became serious enough to interfere with horse racing, the South Carolina Jockey Club agreed to suspend activities
for the duration of the war. Some owners hid their prize horses in swamps to prevent
them from being stolen by the British.

By December 1783, after the war had ended and the British had evacuated
Charleston, the Jockey Club started up again with increased membership, ushering
in the "golden age" of horse racing in South Carolina.

The economic turmoil of the postwar years caused the Jockey Club to disband
twice—in 1788 and in 1791—but each time it re-formed.

In 1791 the primary race course moved once more, when some of the club
members purchased a portion of the Grove Plantation and built the famed one-mile
oval Washington Race Course.

WASHINGTON COURSE, CHARLESTON, S. C.

Engraving of the Washington Race Course by H. Bosse after a daguerreotype by B. Y. Glen,
1857 *Library of Congress*

This course would be considered the epicenter of racing until the late 1800s. Today, the area is known as Hampton Park. The road that circles the park, Mary Murray Boulevard, is built on top of the original racetrack.

Pest House to Vacation Cottage

For most of the eighteenth century, Sullivan's Island was an uninhabited barrier island north of Charleston. Its initial purpose was for quarantine protocol for the port. Ships suspected of carrying infectious diseases were held there for a time, and the crew and passengers were allowed onto the island.

The state legislature suspended the legal importation of African captives into South Carolina in March 1787; however, Sullivan's Island remained the quarantine spot for incoming ships for several more years.

In 1791, the state legislature granted permission for "such citizens of this state as may think it beneficial to their health to reside on Sullivan's Island during the summer season have liberty to build on the said island a dwelling and out houses for their accommodations."

Taking the cue, several wealthy local citizens made their way to the island during the summer of 1791 and began constructing summer cottages.

The first vacationers on Sullivan's Island had to deal with the problem of getting there and transporting supplies. This required owning a boat or hiring a boat and crew. The next year brought a solution with a ferry system from Mount Pleasant.

THE FRENCH ARE COMING!
THE FRENCH ARE COMING!

Two Frenchmen played crucial roles in the formation of the colony and the nation—for different reasons and with different outcomes. Both were welcomed and entertained accordingly.

The "Boy General" Arrives

Having left Bordeaux, France, on March 26, 1777, to "conquer or perish" in the American cause, Marie-Joseph-Paul-Yves-Roch-Gilbert du Motier (also known as the Marquis de Lafayette) navigated in secret for fifty-four days to avoid being captured by the British.

He was successful. He and Baron Johann DeKalb arrived in America at North Island, near Georgetown, about fifty miles north of Charles Town on June 13, 1777. Disembarking from his ship, *La Victoire*, Lafayette called out, "Nous sommes au bord du paradis de Dieu" ("We are on the edge of God's paradise"). The area later became known as DeBordieu.

His party came across Major Benjamin Huger's plantation, where he was invited to stay. Those few nights of hospitality and entertainment cemented a friendship between the two men, which would have long-lasting effects through both their lives and the lives of their descendants.

The party traveled to Charles Town and from there to Philadelphia, where Lafayette met General Washington. Just nineteen at the time, Lafayette was given a commission in the American army as a major-general—earning him the nickname "Boy General"—and he insisted on receiving no pay.

Lafayette played a major role in the war, even commanding the American army that held Cornwallis at Yorktown, Virginia, until Washington could arrive with more troops.

When the war ended in 1783, he returned to France just in time for the French Revolution. His political stance of supporting a constitutional monarchy alienated him from both royalists and radicals. Nevertheless, he became a general at the head of one of the French armies. Later, when the political situation changed and radicals seized the reins of government, Lafayette was declared an enemy of the Revolution and faced the guillotine if he returned to Paris. He fled France and crossed into Austria, where he was captured and imprisoned.

When he was in prison, the person who came to his aid was Dr. Francis Huger of Charleston, son of Lafayette's old friend, Major Benjamin Huger. (The story continues in Section 3: Belle of the Ball.)

Middleton and Michaux

During this time, the gardens at Middleton Place continued to develop. Today they are known as America's oldest surviving landscaped gardens, and they follow the design principles of rational order, geometry, and balance.

Politics played a part in the development of the gardens. Owner Henry Middleton was the second president of the First Continental Congress, and his son, Arthur, was one of the signers of the Declaration of Independence. Arthur's son, Henry (who later, after the Revolutionary War, became a state senator, governor of South Carolina, a member of the US House of Representatives, and a minister to Russia) lived on the property and continued to tend the gardens, which he did with the help of his friend, André Michaux, whom he met through his political connections.

André Michaux was botanist for King Louis XVI. Louis sent him to Charleston in 1785 to catalog and collect plants and trees for the royal nurseries in France. Michaux brought camellias (*camellia japonica*) with him as a house gift when he stayed at Middleton Place. As a result, these became the first camellias grown in an American garden.

Michaux also started a botanical garden of 111 acres on the outskirts of Charleston, where many plants were first introduced to America. Among them were the Persian lilac, the tea plant, the mimosa tree, the chocolate vine, the crape myrtle, the golden fossil tree, and the sweet olive. Michaux also described and named many North American species during this time. Between 1785 and 1791 he shipped ninety cases of plants and many seeds to France.

Michaux's Roots in Versailles

André Michaux was born in Satory, a part of Versailles, where his father managed the farmland on the king's estate. He received a basic education that included Latin and Greek, and he trained in agricultural sciences, assuming he would one day take over his father's duties.

In 1769, he married the daughter of a prosperous farmer. However, one year later she died giving birth to their son, François André. At that point, Michaux began studying botany and collecting specimens in England, Auvergne, the Pyrenees, Spain, and Persia.

His written works include Histoire des chênes de l'Amérique (1801; The Oaks of North America) and Flora Boreali-Americana (1803; The Flora of North America), both of which continued to be botanical references well into the nineteenth century. His son, François André Michaux, also became an authoritative botanist.

WASHINGTON'S TOUR

When Charleston was a colony, the King's birthday was celebrated every year with feasting, fireworks, and military exhibitions. Of course, that holiday disappeared after the American Revolution, but it was replaced by celebrations of George Washington's birthday upon his election as the first federal president in 1789.

In 1791, Washington made a tour of the southern states, and when he arrived in Charleston, the celebration lasted a week.

The tour was, in fact, a public relations move, similar to a trip he made to the New England states to shore up support for the newly created government.

No matter. It was still a celebration for the people of Charleston. And they acted accordingly.

Washington wrote in his diary that by the time he left, he was completely exhausted from his time in Charleston. The people of Charleston would have it no other way.

He crossed the North Carolina–South Carolina border on April 27 and made his way through Horry County, stopping in Georgetown on April 30. The next day he traveled to the Hampton Plantation, owned by the Horry family (daughter of Eliza Lucas Pinckney). After what is described as "an elegant breakfast," he continued his journey, stopping at Awendaw Barony, Joseph Manigault's plantation, for the night. On May 2, he visited Snee Farm, country home of Governor Charles Pinckney, then rode to the ferry landing in what is present-day Mount Pleasant and crossed over to Charleston.

Washington spent more time in Charleston than anywhere else during his southern tour, and the event was documented in great detail in the *Charleston City Gazette* of Saturday, May 14, 1791, showing just how lavish Charlestonians can be when entertaining someone they like.

Here are some excerpts from the write-ups.

Monday, May 2

"On Monday, the second instant, at two o'clock, p.m. the beloved and excellent George Washington, President of the United States of America, arrived in this city, with his suite, to the inexpressible satisfaction as well of strangers as of the citizens. Never, it may be said, were joy, love, affection and esteem more universal upon any one occasion.

"Between 12 and 1 o'clock our amiable president embarked on board an elegant twelve-oared barge prepared for the purpose, and which anxiously waited his arrival at Haddrell's Point, accompanied by Major-General [William] Moultrie, Brigadier-Gen. [Charles Cotesworth] Pinckney, Major Edward Rutledge, Col. [William] Washington, the city recorder [John Bee] in his robes, Col. [John] Dart, and Mr. John Rutledge, jun. This illustriously freighted barge was rowed across Cooper river, from the place of embarkation to Charleston, by thirteen masters of American vessels . . . uniformly and elegantly dressed in close short jackets of light blue silk, black florentine breeches, white silk stockings with light blue silk bow-knots in their shoes, rose-wise; round black hats, with a light blue wide silk sash round the crowns, bearing an elegant impression of the arms of this state, beneath which was this well adapted inscription—'Long Live the President.'

"During the passage on the water, the gentlemen of the Amateur Society [men playing instruments], assisted by [vocalists] Mr. [Job] Palmer, Mr. James Badger, Mr. Jonathan Badger, and Mr. [John Hartley] Harris, with the choir of St. Philip's Church, performed a concert, vocal and instrumental, composed of pieces of music and choruses suited to the joyous occasion. . . . The grand spectacle exhibited by the presidential barge, which was distinguished from the rest by its ornaments, its rowers and the standard [or flag] of the United States, which was displayed at the bow upon a ground of blue silk, accompanied by upwards of forty rowing and sailing boats, filled every joyous, feeling breast ashore with sensations which we will not venture to describe, from a conviction of our being inadequate to the task.

"At Prioleau's Wharf [at the east end of Queen Street] stairs were erected, covered with green cloth, where the president was received on his landing by [Arnoldus Vanderhorst] the Intendant [or mayor] and Wardens [or City Council members] of the city, with their wands [wooden staffs], attended by their officers; also by the governor [Charles Pinckney], lieutenant-governor [Isaac Holmes] and civil officers of the state; with an innumerable concourse of citizens, who welcomed the chief magistrate of the United States with reiterated acclamations—the bells of St. Michael's rang a joyful peal—and the Charleston Battalion of Artillery fired a federal salute. On his landing, the Intendant addressed him [the president] as follows: 'The Intendant and Wardens beg leave, sir, to welcome you to this city. It will be their care to make your stay agreeable. They have provided accommodations for yourself and suite, to which they will be happy to conduct you.' The President replied that he was ready to attend them, and would follow."

The militia company of German Fusiliers, "which was drawn up at the place of landing, then opened their files and enclosed the . . . procession, which moved towards the Exchange, with colors flying, drums beating and fifes playing." During the short walk down East Bay Street, Washington removed his hat and bowed to the left and to the right as he passed through the crowded street.

"Here we must observe, that there was such a concourse of all ranks on board of the several vessels hauled close to the shore, as is almost beyond description. From superannuated old age to lisping infancy the crowd was so great there was scarce room to move. On the illustrious personage's approach to the shore such a buzz of approbation—such a shout of joy took place, as that one must see and hear all to have anything like an adequate idea of it. The shore, the streets, the windows, the balconies—all were so crowded, so beset with spectators, that the most attentive observer must fail in an attempt to do justice to the splendid aspect of the whole.

"Being arrived at the Exchange, the president was conducted to the platform within the grand balustrade of the Exchange, fronting Broad-street, where he stood to await the salutes and discharges from the field artillery disposed and planted for that purpose, as well as to see the order of procession go by in review, when he returned all those salutations of respect which were rendered to him as it passed along.

"The order of procession was then reversed, and the president was escorted up Broad-street, while he with the greatest politeness and attention bowed uncovered [that is, he removed his hat and bowed] to the brilliant assemblage of spectators of both sexes, to the right and to the left . . . till he arrived at the elegant habitation in Church-street destined for his reception, which was ornamented in front by lamps, and over the portal a triumphal arch decorated with laurel, flowers, &c. He there received the warm congratulations of several of the most respectable characters in the state, and was individually introduced to the corporation, the members of the [Society of the] Cincinnati and the officers of the Charleston Battalion of Artillery. At five o'clock he dined with his excellency the governor, at his house in Meeting-street, with a small company of respectable gentlemen."

Tuesday, May 3

President Washington rested at Thomas Heyward's house on Church Street during the first part of the day and later received guests.

"At three o'clock in the afternoon the Intendant and Wardens of this city, attended by their proper officers, waited upon the president, at his house."

The intendant made a brief public address to the president and Washington made a brief cordial reply.

"At half past three o'clock, the merchants [of Charleston] went in a body" to visit the president. Edward Darrell, on behalf of the city's mercantile community, made a brief address to the president, and Washington made a brief, cordial reply.

"At four o'clock the city corporation gave an elegant entertainment to the President of the United States, in the Exchange, which had been recently fitted up and decorated in a very sumptuous style, to which were invited, the governor, lieutenant-governor and officers of the state, union and city, consuls of foreign powers, and reverend clergy, members of the Cincinnati, officers of the militia, gentlemen strangers [that is, gentlemen tourists], and a number of respectable citizens. . . . Over the president's head was fabricated in very ingenious workmanship, a beautiful triumphal arch, from which was suspended a wreath of laurel."

After dinner, the assembled dignitaries and guests drank a series of sixteen toasts, including two by the president: "the State of South Carolina," and "the City of Charleston, and prosperity to it." Outside the walls of the Exchange, "each [toast was] attended by a discharge of cannon from the Charleston Battalion of Artillery. . . . The shipping in the harbor displayed all their colors, throughout the day—and St. Michael's bells echoed forth their joyous peals."

Wednesday, May 4

"Early in the morning, the president, accompanied by [Senator] Mr. [Ralph] Izard, Major-General Moultrie, Brigadier-General Pinckney, Major [Edward] Rutledge and Major [William] Jackson [Washington's secretary], viewed the remains of the lines and batteries which had been thrown up for the defense of the city when attacked by the British fleet and army, under Sir Henry Clinton and Admiral Arbuthnot, in the year 1780: And after riding over the ground on which they had been erected, and reconnoitering the places where the enemy had opened their trenches, placed their batteries, and made their parallels and approaches, he was pleased to express great satisfaction at the very gallant defense that had been made by the garrison during the siege.

"At four o'clock in the afternoon, the Society of the Cincinnati gave a very sumptuous dinner to their illustrious president-general, in McCrady's long-room, which was handsomely embellished with laurel, flowers and shrubbery."

After dinner, the party drank a series of fifteen toasts, each "succeeded by a discharge from the field pieces of the Charleston Battalion of Artillery. A choir of singers entertained the company with several pieces of vocal music, and the day was spent in social festivity.

"In the evening a splendid ball was given by the city corporation at the city hall [in the Exchange], which was elegantly illuminated, furnished and dressed with chaplets of laurel and flowers. The president honored it with his presence, and there was a numerous and brilliant assemblage of ladies and a great number of gentlemen present; the ladies were all elegantly dressed, and most of them wore ribbons and girdles with different inscriptions expressive of their respect and esteem for the president, such as 'Long live the president,'—'He lives the guardian of his country's rights'—'Virtue and valor united'—'Rejoice the hero's come'—Shield, oh! shield him from all harm,' &c. and at proper places, handsome medallions of the president, encircled with spangles and other ornaments. Their fans also exhibited many fanciful and ingenious emblems and inventions, on one of which appeared a representation of Fame crowning the president with a wreath of laurel. Joy, satisfaction and gratitude illumed every countenance and reveled in each heart, whilst the demonstrations of grateful respect shewn him appeared to give him the most heartfelt satisfaction, which visibly displayed itself in his countenance.

"At half past ten, the company sat down to supper; at the table were seated more than 250 ladies, besides gentlemen. The brilliancy of the company and elegance of the supper surpassed all conception. The [German Fusilier] company was drawn up before the Exchange to preserve order, and being in handsome uniform, exhibited a very pleasing appearance: In short, every circumstance of the evening's entertainment was truly picturesque of the most pleasing elegance."

The president's tour continued for five more action-packed days during which Washington was wined and dined and praised at every opportunity. By Monday, May 9, he and his entourage headed north through the Charleston Neck area and crossed the Ashley River.

> Went to a concert where there were 400 ladies, the number and appearance of which exceeded anything I had ever seen.
> —Washington, writing in his journal about some of the entertainment he found in Charleston

Washington's Architect

George Washington's visit to Charleston netted an important find for the president.

During the visit, as the civic leaders gave the president a tour of the most important buildings, Washington was introduced to architect James Hoban, who had moved to the city only a few years before.

A year later, commissioners in charge of designing the new capital city of Washington announced that they would receive proposals for a residence befitting the country's chief executive, as well as a capitol building for Congress.

Hoban was specifically invited to submit drawings and traveled from Charleston to Philadelphia to discuss matters with President Washington. On the day of the design competition review, held in Washington on July 16, 1792, the president immediately selected Hoban's plan.

SEE FOR YOURSELF: REVOLUTIONARY PERIOD

When you're in town, be sure to see where history was made during the Revolutionary period with these tours.

The Charleston Museum: Then and Now

Founded in 1773, the Charleston Museum is America's first museum and has its own interesting history. It was created by the Charleston Library Society, and Charles Cotesworth Pinckney and Thomas Heyward Jr. were both early curators.

Before visiting the existing museum, it's worth a look at the site of the previous museum building on Rutledge Avenue.

In its early years, the museum's collection moved around to different locations:

- On the upper floors of the Charleston County Courthouse at Meeting and Broad Streets—an intersection known as the "Four Corners of Law."
- Housed in the Medical College of South Carolina (the forerunner to today's Medical University of South Carolina) on Queen Street near Franklin Street. (The site today is residential.)
- On the upper floor of the College of Charleston's Randolph Hall.

In 1907 the museum found its first independent home at the Thomas Auditorium at the corner of Rutledge and Calhoun Streets.

CANNON PARK: OLD MUSEUM RUINS AND HARLESTON GREEN

131 Rutledge Ave.

In 1980, the museum moved to its current location on Meeting Street. A year later, this structure was destroyed in a fire. Afterward, this area was converted into a park and greenspace.

In the early 1700s, this area was known as Harleston Green, site of the first golf course in America. (For more info on Harleston Green and the evolution of golf in the area, see page pages 30, 59, and 96.)

CHARLESTON MUSEUM

360 Meeting St.

The Museum features two levels of exhibits that show the history of Charleston and the Lowcountry with hundreds of artifacts. The first level is home to the Natural History section, temporary exhibits that focus on local history, and the museum's gift shop. The second level is home to several permanent exhibits:

- Lowcountry History Hall—exhibits about the Native Americans who first inhabited the area as well as the first colonists and the enslaved African Americans who transformed the region into an agricultural empire

- The Armory—displays of historic weaponry

- Becoming Americans and Charleston in the Civil War—showcasing

The Charleston Museum by Frances Benjamin Johnston, 1937 *Point North Images*

Charleston's role in the American Revolution and the Civil War

- Early Days—exhibits from the museum's beginnings, including collections from around the world
- Kidstory—an interactive exhibit of Charleston history for children
- Historic Textiles—rotating exhibits from the museum's historic textiles and clothing collection
- Charleston Silver—a display of the South's finest silver craftsmen and women

The museum also owns two historic homes—the Joseph Manigault House (located across the street from the museum) and the Heyward-Washington House (on Church Street)—both open to the public.

Michaux's Landscape Work

MIDDLETON PLACE

4300 Ashley River Rd., Charleston, 29414
https://www.middletonplace.org/

Middleton Place, known today as America's oldest surviving landscaped gardens, were developed thanks to the help of André Michaux, botanist for King Louis XVI. Louis sent him to Charleston in 1785 to catalog and collect plants and trees for the royal nurseries in France. Michaux brought as a house gift to Middleton Place some camellias (*camellia japonica*), which became the first camellias grown in an American garden. (For more info on Michaux, see page 63.)

The gardens at Middleton Place follow the design principles of rational order, geometry, and balance—and in the gardens, something is always in bloom.

The site's 110 acres include sixty-five acres of gardens, floral allees, ornamental butterfly-shaped lakes, terraced lawns, a house museum, working stableyards, a restaurant, an inn, and an organic farm.

In the spring and fall, Middleton Place hosts evening strolls and wine tours.

While you're in the area, visit these two other plantation sites, which are a few yards down the road.

MAGNOLIA GARDENS

3550 Ashley River Rd., Charleston, 29414
https://magnoliaplantation.com/

Open to the public since 1870, Magnolia Plantation and Gardens contains the oldest public gardens in America.

Tourists from around the world have come to Magnolia to view the gardens, which, in some sections, are more than 325 years old, making them the oldest unrestored gardens in America. The plantation has been under the ownership of the same family for more than three centuries, with each generation adding its own personal touch, expanding the gardens and adding to the variety of specimens.

Admission includes access to the grounds and historic gardens, the conservatory, the petting zoo and nature center, the horticulture maze, and the wildlife observation tower. Guided tours have additional fees. The site also includes a cafe that serves beverages, snacks, and lunch and the Gilliard Garden Center, where you can purchase and take home some of Magnolia's plants, herbs, and shrubs.

Formal Gardens: considered the last large-scale romantic gardens left in the country. Unlike other gardens in America, which are formal and seek to control nature, Magnolia cooperates with nature to create an appealing landscape.

Children's Garden: located just past the plantation house, the garden includes a fairy garden with gnomes, elves, and woodland creatures in a fairytale setting; a village with small-scale houses and buildings; and a sensory garden where the kids can see, smell, touch, taste, and hear.

Plantation House Tour: a half-hour guided tour of the third Drayton Family home to occupy the site. Ten rooms are open to the public and are furnished with early-American items as well as family heirlooms.

Magnolia Cabin Project Tour: a forty-five-minute guided tour that highlights a project to preserve five historic structures: four cabins built in the 1850s and a smokehouse built circa 1900. The tour focuses on the history of slavery at Magnolia and the lives of the enslaved families. After the Civil War, these cabins were inhabited by free men and women who worked to design and maintain the gardens and served as the first tour guides.

Nature Tram Tour: every half-hour trams tour the plantation's forest, lakes, marshes, and wetlands. The forty-five-minute guided tour includes views of nineteenth-century rice ponds, Native American ceremonial mounds, a row of slave cabins, and six hundred acres of wildlife habitats and gardens.

Nature Boat Tour: a forty-five-minute tour similar to the Nature Tram Tour but viewed from the water.

Zoo and Nature Center: a chance to interact with domestic animals that are representative of plantation life. Exhibits show indigenous species, including white-tailed deer, gray fox, beaver, bobcat, and birds of prey. A reptile house has native specimens, including some that are venomous.

Audubon Swamp Garden: located on the exit road, on the left before leaving the plantation. Boardwalks, bridges, and dikes allow you to explore native plants and wildlife on your own.

Sunday Bird Walks: a docent-led tour held the first Sunday of every month.

DRAYTON HALL
3380 Ashley River Rd., Charleston, 29414
https://www.draytonhall.org/
Drayton Hall is the only plantation house on the Ashley River to survive intact through both the Revolutionary and Civil Wars and was declared a National Historic Landmark in 1960.

The eighteenth-century plantation is considered an outstanding example of Palladian architecture in North America. The South Carolina Department of Archives and History claims that Drayton Hall is "without question one of the finest of all surviving plantation houses in America."

Drayton Hall is also an active archaeological site with an extensive museum collection of rare eighteenth- and nineteenth-century objects and artifacts. Because Drayton Hall has never been restored, the house provides an opportunity to study materials and designs from every period in the house's history.

The mansion was built for John Drayton Sr. (1715–1779) after he bought the property in 1738. He was born at what is now Magnolia Plantation and Gardens, but as the third son in his family, he was unlikely to inherit his birthplace.

The house sits on a 630-acre plat that is part of the plantation based on indigo and rice. The site formerly included thirteen slave cabins believed to have housed approximately seventy-eight slaves.

Drayton Hall *Library of Congress*

Seven generations of Draytons preserved the house in all but original condition, though the laundry house did not survive the 1886 earthquake and a hurricane destroyed the kitchen in 1893.

Drayton Hall is owned by the National Trust for Historic Preservation and managed by the Drayton Hall Preservation Trust, which opened the house to the public in 1976.

The main house tour is an audio tour (you may bring earphones or earbuds or purchase them onsite). Guides are stationed throughout the house to answer questions. An interpreter-led one-hour house tour is also available at 9:00. There are no extra fees to tour the landscape or visit Drayton Hall's museum galleries.

The landscape presents an eighteenth-century gentleman's country seat. John Drayton used existing trees and native plants in his garden, and the landscape was further embellished with exotic plants by his son, Charles Drayton.

The Lenhardt Garden, located in the Visitors Center, is a semi-formal courtyard garden anchored under a live oak that was likely planted around 1800, a display of Charles Drayton's interest in botany.

Walking Tour of Washington's Visit

Many of the landmarks from Washington's visit are still standing and, in some cases, open for tours.

Start where Washington started: on East Bay Street at the Exchange Building.

THE OLD EXCHANGE & PROVOST DUNGEON

122 East Bay St.

Washington reached Charleston early on the afternoon of May 2. Soon after he landed, he addressed the city from the Old Exchange Building. At that time, the building served as Charleston's City Hall and the city's premier gathering place. During the first banquet, Washington's table was on the main floor, roughly where the gift shop is today.

The Old Exchange & Provost Dungeon holds tours that includes the Provost Dungeon, where you can see a wax figure of pirate Stede Bonnet (see page 39).

From the Old Exchange Building, head south (toward the Battery) two blocks to Tradd Street. (You will pass Rainbow Row, the iconic group of pastel-colored houses, on the right.) Turn right onto Tradd Street and go two blocks to Church Street and turn right. The Heyward-Washington House will be on the left.

HEYWARD-WASHINGTON HOUSE

87 Church St.

Washington did, in fact, sleep here.

When word of the president's visit reached the city, everyone wanted to offer him lodging. The consummate politician, Washington left the decision to city leaders, who chose the town home of Thomas Heyward Jr.

Heyward, a signer of the Declaration of Independence, Revolutionary patriot, and militia officer, had owned the house for many years, but by 1791, he lived at his plantation house, which meant the house was available during the president's stay.

Washington took up residence and actually paid for his own room. On May 3, a contingent of "respectable ladies of Charleston" held a drop-in at the house, and the next day, he received visitors there. In his diary, he described the accommodations as, "very good."

Tours are available through the Charleston Museum.

Heyward Washington House *Point North Images*

From the Heyward-Washington House, continue on Church Street (heading toward Broad Street) to St. Michael's Alley (about a block) on the left. Take the alley to Meeting Street and turn right, where St. Michael's Episcopal Church is on the right.

As you walk by the graveyard, notice the marker on the wall noting that a couple of signers of the Constitution are buried there.

ST. MICHAEL'S EPISCOPAL CHURCH

71 Broad St.

On Sunday, May 8, Washington attended two worship services— one at this church and one at St. Philip's (which you will see later in this tour). He climbed to the top of the steeple to admire the view of the city. (Note: The church no longer allows public access to the steeple.)

Here, he sat in pew 43, which originally had been known as "The Governor's Pew." The pews have remained the same through the years, and, though pew 43 no longer has a plaque designating where Washington sat, it is located in the middle section of pews near the front.

From here, go up Broad Street a block and a half to the John Rutledge House.

St. Michael's Episcopal Church *Point North Images*

JOHN RUTLEDGE HOUSE

116 Broad St.

Washington did not sleep here—he was a guest at the Heyward House for his entire stay in Charleston—but he did have breakfast at this location.

The John Rutledge House *Point North Images*

Now known as the John Rutledge House Inn, the bed and breakfast has been updated, of course, but the building still retains the inlaid floors, plaster molding, and elaborate ironwork from its earlier days.

From here, go back down Broad Street to the corner of Broad and Meeting Street, on the other side of the street from St. Michael's Church. This intersection is known as "The Four Corners of Law"—so named because of the buildings on the corners: Federal Post Office, State Courthouse, City Hall, and Church (God's law). Here you'll visit the council chambers inside City Hall.

CHARLESTON CITY HALL

80 Broad St.

Washington did not visit this location—because it didn't exist at the time he was here—but the wall of City Council chambers holds a souvenir of Washington's visit.

Next door is Washington Square Park.

Charleston City Hall *Point North Images*

The city commissioned John Trumbull, the famous Revolutionary War artist, to paint a portrait of the president to commemorate his visit. Trumbull set the painting on the eve of the Battle of Princeton. When the Charlestonians saw it, they sent it back asking for a painting of Washington in Charleston.

Though he wasn't happy about it, Trumbull painted it again, this time showing Washington at Haddrells Point, where he took the ferry across the Cooper River, and Charleston is in the background. Trumbull included Washington's white horse in the painting—with the horse's rear the dominant feature. (It's believed Trumbull did this on purpose to let the people of Charleston know what he thought of them.)

WASHINGTON SQUARE PARK
74 Broad St.
This park is another location that didn't exist during Washington's visit—at that time, the space was occupied by Corbett's Thatched Tavern—but as it's dedicated to our first president, the half-block of greenspace is worth a visit.

The park contains a number of historical monuments and statues (more details on page 143), including a miniature version of the Washington Monument in the center, which pays tribute to the Washington Light Infantry.

Make your way through the park to Chalmers Street—one of the remaining cobblestone roads in the city—and after one block, turn left onto Church Street and go two blocks (crossing Queen Street) to St. Philip's Church.

ST. PHILIP'S CHURCH

142 Church St.

Washington also worshipped at this church. Several of the signers of the Declaration of Independence were members, so his choice to visit two churches might have been more political than spiritual. The building was destroyed by fire and rebuilt, so the specific pew where he sat is unknown.

Go back down Church Street and turn left onto Queen Street (beside the French Huguenot Church). Go a block to State Street and turn right. Roughly halfway down State Street, turn left onto Unity Alley.

MCCRADY'S TAVERN AND RESTAURANT

2 Unity Alley

McCrady's dates back to 1778, when it was a tavern and later a restaurant (see page 53 for more details). In 1791, the Society of the Cincinnati hosted a thirty-course banquet dinner party for Washington in its long room. The evening's festivities included performance by a choral group, and the Charleston Artillery fired volleys outside after each of the fifteen toasts made that night.

McCrady's Tavern in present day *Point North Images*

SECTION 3:
THE BELLE OF THE BALL

Antebellum Period, 1792–1860

The Charleston races are the most popular, the most fashionable and the best attended of any in the United States. Race week, in that city, has been aptly termed "the Carnival" of South Carolina—the annual jubilee of the State. The reason is perfectly obvious; the course and its appointments are under the control of gentlemen of the highest character, and nothing is permitted to interfere with the legitimate sports of the Turf, which are managed with a degree of spirit, liberality, and scrupulous propriety unknown elsewhere on this side of the Atlantic.

—WILLIAM T. PORTER, A NEWSPAPERMAN AND SECRETARY OF THE NEW YORK JOCKEY CLUB, WRITING IN 1840 ABOUT CHARLESTON'S RACING SOCIETY.

Timeline Highlights: 1792–1860

Elsewhere		Charleston
1793: Louis XVI and Marie Antoinette executed. Reign of Terror in France begins. Napoleon takes Toulon. 1793: Building of the Capitol in Washington, DC, begins. 1793: Jardin des Plantes museum opens in Paris, later becomes first zoo. 1794: John Trumbull paints "The Declaration of Independence." 1794: US Navy established. 1794: "Auld Lang Syne" published by Burns. 1795: Paris Conservatoire de Musique founded. 1798: US Marine Corps established. 1799: Rosetta Stone found in Egypt	1792–1799	1792: Washington Race Course ready by Race Week. 1793: Charleston Theatre (Broad Street Theatre) opens. 1794: Charleston French Theatre opens. 1795: Vauxhall Garden opens. 1797: First ice house opens. 1798: First advertisements for ice cream. 1799: Yellow fever outbreak in city.
1800: All US federal offices moved from Philadelphia to Washington, DC. 1800: Library of Congress established. 1804: Napoleon proclaimed emperor of France. 1804: Burr-Hamilton duel mortally wounds Hamilton. 1807: US Embargo Act against Britain and France. 1807: US Congress passes Slave Trade Act prohibiting importation of slaves.	1800	1801: Hibernian Society founded. 1806: Franklin Library Society founded. 1807: Washington Light Infantry founded.

Elsewhere		Charleston
1807: First Ascot Gold Cup in England. 1808: Excavations begin at Pompeii. 1809: The Two Thousand Guineas established at Newmarket Races in England.		
1812–1814: United States at war with Britain. 1814: Francis Scott Key writes poem that will later become "Star-Spangled Banner." 1815: Napoleon defeated at Waterloo. 1817: New York Stock Exchange founded. 1818: First performance of "Stille Nacht, Heilige Nacht (Silent Night, Holy Night)" in Austria. 1819: Opening of Burlington Arcade in Piccadilly.	1810	1813: Literary and Philosophical Society of South Carolina founded. 1813: Ladies Benevolent Society founded. 1818: Samuel Morse, inventor of telegraph, arrives in Charleston to begin printing business.
1820: Keats writes "Ode to a Nightingale"; Scott writes *Ivanhoe*; Shelley writes *Prometheus Unbound*. 1821: Ecole de Chartres founded in Paris. 1822: Royal Academy of Music in London founded. 1823: Charles Macintosh of Scotland sells the first raincoat. 1824: National Gallery in London opens to the public.	1820	1822: Alleged slave uprising attempt by Denmark Vesry and others; thirty-five are hanged. 1824: Founding of Medical College of South Carolina (later Medical University of South Carolina), first medical school in the South. 1825: Lafayette visits Charleston again.

Elsewhere		Charleston
1825: Buckingham Palace built. 1825: The *Diary of Samuel Pepys* published. 1828: Dumas writes *The Three Musketeers.* 1829: First Oxford-Cambridge boat race.		1828–1829: Edgar Allan Poe stationed at Fort Moultrie on Sullivan's Island.
1831: London Bridge completed. 1831: Great Cholera pandemic spreads through Asia and Europe. 1834: Hugo publishes *The Hunchback of Notre Dame.* 1835: Hans C. Andersen begins publishing stories for children. 1835: P. T. Barnum begins his career as a showman. 1837: Victoria becomes queen of Great Britain. 1837: Morse displays his electric telegraph invention. 1839: First baseball game at Cooperstown, NY	1830	1830: Train passenger service begins between Charleston and Hamburg, SC, with "The Best Friend of Charleston" steam locomotive. 1831: Audubon arrives in Charleston and begins work on his book, *Birds of America.* 1837: White Point Garden designated a public park. 1838: Osceola, chief of Seminoles, dies during imprisonment at Fort Moultrie. 1838: Great Fire of 1838 destroys much of Ansonborough neighborhood.
1843: First nightclub, "Le Bal des Anglais," opens in Paris. 1843: Dickens publishes *A Christmas Carol.* 1844: Dumas publishes *The Count of Monte Cristo.* 1845: Poe publishes "The Raven."	1840	1840: A public bathing house is constructed at the battery, with a cake and ice cream parlor on top. 1842: The Citadel (Military College of South Carolina) is founded. First class of cadets is held the following year.

Elsewhere		Charleston
1845: Annapolis Naval School (later US Naval Academy) opens. 1846–1848: Mexican-American War. 1847: Charlotte Bronte publishes *Jane Eyre*. 1847: Emily Bronte publishes *Wuthering Heights*. 1847: Thackeray publishes *Vanity Fair*. 1848: Gold is discovered in California.		1843: Poe publishes "The Gold-Bug," set on Sullivan's Island. 1843: W. T. Sherman stationed at Fort Moultrie.
1850: Paxton builds Crystal Palace in London. 1851: Great Exhibition opens in London. 1852: Stowe publishes *Uncle Tom's Cabin*. 1852: First Harvard-Yale regatta. 1853: Henry Steinway and sons begin piano manufacturing company in New York. 1854: Thoreau publishes *Walden; or, Life in the Woods*. 1855: Paris World Fair held. 1858: Royal Opera House opens in Covent Garden, London. 1859: Darwin publishes *On the Origin of Species*.	1850	1852: Construction of the Big Brick is completed. 1853: Mills House Hotel completed. 1855: South Carolina Historical Society founded. 1855: Planter's Hotel sold and renamed Calder's Inn. 1858: Carolina Art Association chartered by General Assembly.

Elsewhere	1860	Charleston
1860: British Open Golf Championship starts. 1860: Abraham Lincoln wins Republican Party presidential nomination (and later the presidency). 1860: First sound recording of a human voice on a "phonautograph machine."		1860: Lincoln's election prompts the resignation of federal officials in the city. 1860: Ordinance of Secession ratified at Institute Hall, proclaiming South Carolina "an independent commonwealth."

FLORA, FAUNA, AND THE ICE AGE

In the Antebellum Period, Charleston was at her most regal. The trees and shrubbery planted during the colonial and Revolutionary eras were coming to full growth, and the entire area was a magnificent decoration outdoors.

White Point Garden and The Battery

Located in the heart of Charleston's historic district, White Point Garden provides a view of Fort Sumter, Castle Pinckney, the Sullivan's Island Lighthouse, and Charleston Harbor—where, as the locals say, "the Ashley and Cooper rivers meet to form the Atlantic Ocean."

The garden, also known as Battery Park, is a 5.7-acre space at the southernmost tip of the Charleston peninsula. The key streets of Meeting, King, and Church end at White Point Garden. From the early years, this area was known as Oyster Point because of the oyster shells left from years of oyster harvesting and shucking.

Initially the area was used for military purposes. A watch tower was built there in the late 1680s, and within a few years, local cannons and entrenchments were added as well.

By the early 1700s, the name changed to White Point, so named for the white oyster shells and the white sands along the beach. In 1737, Broughton's Battery (also known as Fort Wilkins) was built on the site. In the 1750s, a seawall was constructed alongside White Point, and in 1789 the fort was demolished and decommissioned.

The area remained a military outpost for a few more years, then became private residences. When a new wall and promenade were completed, it was still called The Battery—and continues to be called that today.

The City of Charleston purchased the White Point area and in 1837 made it a public park.

In 1840, a public bathing house was constructed on the battery, with a cake and ice cream parlor on top of the building.

A few years later, Mrs. Martha Carrington, who lived at 2 Meeting Street—on the edge of the park—built a gazebo in the center of White Point Garden in honor of her parents. The bandstand was the site of summer band concerts for almost a century.

The Battery and Sea Wall, circa 1900 *Library of Congress*

East Battery, South Carolina postcard *Courtesy of South Caroliniana Library, University of South Carolina, SC*

Audubon and Bachman—
the Convergence of Science and Religion

In 1831, John James Audubon traveled to Charleston to find and paint southern birds. He befriended naturalist John Bachman, the pastor of St. John's Lutheran Church. During the 1830s, Audubon made Bachman's home the center of his work.

Bachman was the pastor of St. John's Lutheran in Charleston for fifty-six years. During that time, he also studied natural history and was a proponent of secular and religious education. He helped found Newberry College and the Lutheran Theological Southern Seminary, as well as the South Carolina Lutheran Synod.

The two men worked together on two important works: The Birds of America *and* Viviparous Quadrupeds of North America.

Charleston's Ice Age

In 1797, Jeremiah Jessop, hoping to stand out in the hotel business, built Charleston's first ice house and began importing ice from the northern states. By summer of 1798, he began selling a new product called ice cream from his shop on Broad Street.

Ice cream was not a new invention, but it was new to the people of Charleston. In fact, it was so new that many people were afraid to try it, believing that consuming cold refreshments in warm weather was harmful. Jessop took to the paper to reassure them.

"To relieve them of such apprehensions," he wrote in the *City Gazette* of 4 June 1798, "he assures them they [ice creams] may be taken with safety in the greatest state of perspiration; for it is only the rawness of any cold substance which is injurious; and as the creams are composed wholly of nourishing substances, and those boiled before they are frozen, they are the most pleasant and nourishing refreshment that can be taken in a warm climate."

Apparently his reassurances worked. He began selling ice cream by the bowl at his Broad Street shop and by the pound for home use. He also sold raw ice, advertising that it was beneficial "for cooling butter in the morning, or other purposes in the course of the day."

By the next year, he advertised another specialty: iced punch mixed with liquors and fruits, which he also sold to the other hotels. However, despite the popularity of the frozen products, Jessop's business faltered, and his ice house was sold at auction in late 1799.

Over the next few years, several other entrepreneurs marketed ice cream to Charlestonians during the summer, with flavors such as raspberry, pineapple, vanilla, and orange-flower.

Imports of ice from New England were stalled prior to and during the War of 1812; however, several investors came to Charleston and constructed several ice houses on the waterfront. This kept Charlestonians supplied with ice until the start of the Civil War.

RECAPTURING THE GLORY DAYS: ART, SPORT, AND THEATER

Indoors or outdoors, when it came to entertainment and leisure, *tradition* was the focus for Charleston. The city had established herself in the early days as refined, cultured, and the epitome of entertainment, and now that the war was over and postwar recovery was well underway, it was time to recapture that golden time.

It was time to focus on art, sport, and theater.

Carolina Art Association

Organized by a group of prominent planters and other supporters, the Carolina Art Association (CAA) of Charleston was officially chartered by the General Assembly on December 21, 1858—before the organizations that established the Museum of Fine Arts in Boston and the Metropolitan Museum of New York.

Its purpose was to promote fine arts throughout the state with exhibitions and to create a permanent collection. The first exhibition was held the following April at the Apprentices Library Society on Horlbeck Alley, displaying 176 works borrowed from private collections in the city.

During the first three years, the CAA held an annual exhibition, and its membership grew steadily, as did its funding. Besides the $10 annual membership dues, the CAA held a fair in May 1859 that raised $6,000, which allowed it to invest in a permanent collection and commission its first piece, *Sergeant Jasper Raising the Flag at Fort Moultrie* by Emmanuel Leutze, a German-born American painter.

IN DEFENSE OF ART

In 1859, at a celebration of the first anniversary of the Carolina Art Association, held at the Hibernian Hall, Nathaniel Russell Middleton—at that time president of the College of Charleston and later president of the CAA—gave a speech about the value as well as the practicality of art. His words were as impassioned as they were scholarly, given that society was in the midst of the Industrial Revolution.

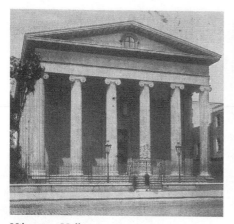

Hibernian Hall *Courtesy of South Caroliniana Library, University of South Carolina, SC*

Hibernian Hall gates *Library of Congress*

"We need not complain that steam and machinery and improved instrumentalities have defrauded the laborer of his support, when his demand for employment is met by awakening him to higher and more intellectual pursuits, and compelling him to search his own divinely endowed nature for mines of dormant wealth and regions of hidden beauty," Middleton said. "Can there be any doubt, that, as military ability has often been indebted for its germination and development to the throes and convulsions of agonized nations, so the world may now be teeming with artists of divine endowment, whose fire-baptism can only be accomplished under the most stringent application of the law of supply and demand?"

Golf

Between 1795—when an announcement in the *South Carolina Gazette* noted "the GOLF CLUB will be held on Saturday next at the Club house on Harleston's Green"—and the last known announcement of the club's meeting in October 1799, the South Carolina Golf Club flourished.

The Golf Club disappeared from historical record after 1799, and golf in the area waned in the 1800s, most likely because of Thomas Jefferson's Embargo Act of 1807, which caused a decline in commercial trading with Great Britain, especially with the Charleston merchants.

In the 1800s, Harleston Green gradually became a neighborhood, with homes built on the former course. The sport was revived in the 1900s with two magnificent courses at Belvidere Golf Links and the Charleston Country Club. (See Section 4: The Late Unpleasantness and Section 5: Doing the Charleston for more on the golf scene.)

The Jockey Club

After the Revolutionary War, racing started up again with enthusiasm, and the South Carolina Jockey Club was immersed in the "golden age of racing."

The Jockey Club moved from the New Market course (in present-day North Charleston) closer to downtown on a parcel of land purchased from the Grove Farm. The new location, Washington Race Course, featured a one-mile loop that became one of the most popular tracks in the South. The new course was ready by Race Week in February 1792.

Every year, for one exciting week in February, the Washington Race Course came to life with racing on Wednesday through Saturday. Schools were let out and businesses imposed a holiday on their employees—with the exception of tavern-keepers, who rented houses nearby to set up restaurants, bars, and inns. Most daily life customs were put on hold while all attention was diverted to the races.

The races became a common meeting place for planters not only from across the state but also from Virginia, Georgia, Kentucky, and Louisiana. The races drew interest from breeders across the region who wanted entry into the competition. Spectators came from as far away as New York, with ships arriving daily for Race Week.

Theatrical Venues

After the Dock Street Theatre burned in 1740, two playhouses were constructed: the New Theatre in 1754 and the Church Street Theatre in 1773, to replace the New Theatre. The latter burned in 1782.

The well-to-do plantation owners spent half the year in the city living a social life, so theater was a major part of life for the Charleston planter-based aristocracy.

Hence the construction of a new theater with, for the first time, a permanent staff.

BROAD STREET THEATRE (CHARLESTON THEATRE)

In 1792, Thomas Wade West and his partner, John Bignall, announced plans for a new theater to house a company of performers managed by West. The building was designed by James Hoban, best known as the architect of the White House in Washington (see Washington's Architect in Section 2: Becoming America).

The *City Gazette* of August 14, 1792, reported "the ground was laid off for the new theatre, on Savage's Green. . . . 125 feet in length, the width 56 feet, the height 37 feet, with a handsome pediment, stone ornaments, a large flight of stone steps, and a courtyard palisaded."

Broad Street Theatre, also called Charleston Theatre, opened in February 1793, midway through the social season, with dramas, dancing, and music. The twelve-hundred-seat theatre operated between 1793 and 1833, under various ownerships.

The theater's orchestra players also served the St. Cecilia Society, so the schedules of that concert series and the theater were coordinated. The society used the building for their concerts until 1817.

CHARLESTON FRENCH THEATRE (THEATRE FRANCAIS)

Within a year of the Charleston Theatre's opening, John Sollée opened a French-language theater on Church Street called the Charleston French Theatre or Theatre Francais. The inaugural performance on April 21, 1794, featured the comedy, *Harlequin Robbed*, along with singing and tightrope dancing.

A fierce competition developed between the two theaters and grew even worse with political divisions over the war between France and Great Britain. For the most part, the wealthy elite were patrons of the Shakespearian productions at the Charleston Theatre, whereas the Jacobin revolutionaries preferred the comedies, acrobatics, and light opera presented at the French Theatre.

VAUXHALL GARDEN

The original Vauxhall Garden, opened in 1661 in London beside the Thames River, was a pleasure garden where patrons paid an entry fee to enjoy walks, refreshments, and entertainment.

The name carried into the new world in the form of tea gardens in New York, Philadelphia, and Charleston.

The first Charleston Vauxhall Garden was a concert and dining venue on Broad Street, operated by "Citizen Cornet." It opened in 1795 with French music, supper, and refreshments. Advertisements in the newspaper noted that tickets were $2 "for each gentleman, accompanied or not by ladies." During the winter social season, the venue held a ball (sometimes masked) along with supper every Friday evening.

When a fire ravaged much of Broad Steet in 1796, Cornet gave up the business and returned to his previous occupation of piano and harpsichord tuning and repair.

The building was unharmed by the fire, however, and restauranteur William Robinson took over the lease, renamed it, and turned it into a gentlemen's dining room and tavern. The venue had limited success and eventually closed.

In June 1799, the name Vauxhall rose to prominence again when French-born Alexander Placide and his wife, English-born Charlotte Wrighten, established a pleasure garden at the corner of Broad and Friend (now Legare) Streets.

The couple brought with them a great deal of experience in the entertainment field. Placide was an acrobat, actor, dancer, theater impresario, and tightrope walker, and his wife was an actress and singer. Together they managed a troupe that performed at the French Theatre on Church Street and later at the Broad Street Theatre. Their company made regular trips to other southern cities during the winter and to northern resorts in the summer months when Charleston's theater was closed.

Now, with the establishment of Vauxhall Garden, Placide was able to fill the gap in summer entertainment with a variety of programs at the pleasure garden.

On July 1, 1799, the *South-Carolina State Gazette* reported about the venue: "Benches and other convenient seats will be put in every proper point, and cold suppers prepared at a minute's warning. The doors will open at half past seven and be shut at eleven o'clock. Price, half a dollar."

During the summer, Placide began offering concerts at Vauxhall, with theater vocalists who had remained in Charleston through the offseason. In fact, because they found employment at Vauxhall Gardens, many performers opted to stay in Charleston and make the city their permanent residence.

Over the next few years, Placide made a series of improvements on the garden:

When Vauxhall Garden opened for the summer in May 1800, advertisements noted that "the days on which there will be no Vauxhall, the garden will be illuminated for those ladies and gentlemen who wish to take ice cream and refreshments until 10 o'clock in the evening."

In 1801, evening concerts ended with fireworks.

By 1802, Placide had put together a small orchestra that offered ongoing concerts with singers from the Charleston Theatre's retinue.

In 1804, he installed bathing facilities, offering either warm or cold baths. The baths were open daily from 6:00 a.m. to 10:00 p.m. at 50 cents each, with discounts of three for a dollar for regular patrons. (These rates continued over the next decade, when different proprietors carried on the Vauxhall bath, garden, and entertainment businesses separately.)

Placide died during a trip to New York in the summer of 1812. A few months after his death and at the invitation of his widow, managers of the New York, Philadelphia, and Baltimore Circus—known as the Olympic Theatre—constructed an amphitheater behind the Vauxhall Garden, with entrances on both Broad and Queen Streets, which offered box seats and standing room in the pit. The first show featured eight-horse cavalry maneuvers, daredevil riding, and a clown from the Theatre Royal in London who performed feats of buffoonery and horsemanship. The evening concluded with fireworks.

Placide's widow operated the Vauxhall property for only a few seasons. In February 1816, the land, amphitheater, stable, and other fixtures were sold at auction. Over the next five years, the land was resold several times, but the baths continued to open every spring.

In 1821, the Right Reverend Dr. John England, the first Roman Catholic Bishop of Charleston, arrived to take up his duties over the diocese of the Carolinas and Georgia. He purchased the property for the diocese and built a small wooden building while he planned a larger cathedral. Today's Cathedral of St. John the Baptist occupies the site of Vauxhall Gardens.

The circus site behind the property was refurbished years later, with a removable stage and forestage installed.

BROAD STREET THEATRE AND CHARLESTON FRENCH THEATRE MERGER: CITY THEATRE, CONCERT HALL, THE THEATRE

By the end of the 1795–1796 season, the Broad Street Theatre was out of business, and West sold it to Sollée, who united the two venues.

The two companies merged in the spring and offered several benefit performances, with proceeds going to various performers or charitable causes like the Charleston Orphan House.

Through the summer of 1796, the theater on Church Street stayed open under the name, "City Theatre," while the Broad Street house remained dark.

Finally, by the spring of 1800, both playhouses were open, with the Broad Street venue offering drama and the Church Street presenting music, acrobatics, and ballet.

After 1800, Sollée allocated the Church Street venue as music hall and ball-room—known for years as "Concert Hall"—leaving the Broad Street Theatre as Charleston's only playhouse, referred to simply as "The Theatre."

In the remaining years of both venues, a different kind of drama played out.

The theater closed when the War of 1812 broke out and reopened in 1815 under new management, followed by a succession of managers, none of whom were adept at business. One lost the lease on the Broad Street Theatre due to debts and lawsuits and was jailed for a brief time. His tenure also saw the Charleston Theatre Riot of 1817, in which the audience sided with the actor in his conflict with management.

And yet, all was not bad. During this time, President James Monroe visited Charleston's theater in 1819, and Junius Brutus Booth (father of actor Edwin Booth and soon-to-be presidential assassin John Wilkes Booth) performed several engagements in the winter of 1821–1822.

The theater deteriorated during the early 1820s, and a new owner reopened in February 1826 with new scenery and pageants. He brought the New-York and Philadelphia Company of Equestrians and its twenty horses to the city, and they performed at the circus facility behind the Vauxhall Garden. Later the horses appeared on stage during the "grand drama of the Cataract of the Ganges." He also brought the Shakespearian works *King Lear*, *Othello*, and *Richard III* back to Charleston.

By 1832, attendance fell, attributed to the steep price of tickets at a time when Charleston's economy was weakened.

The theater closed permanently on July 25, 1833, with no fanfare or eulogy for the establishment. Only a small notice in the *Southern Patriot* marked the occasion: "The building at the west end of Broad Street, called the Charleston Theatre, has been purchased by the faculty of the Medical College of the State of South Carolina for the sum of $12,000. It will be fitted up for the classes attached to this institution."

NEW CHARLESTON THEATRE

After the Broad Street Theatre, Charleston's only purpose-built playhouse, closed in 1832, the city was without a proper theatrical venue. Many of the visiting performers, including international star Tyrone Power, had to perform in the refurbished circus amphitheater beside the old Vauxhall Garden.

To the cultured and entertainment-loving Charlestonians, that just wouldn't do.

In early 1835, Robert Witherspoon stepped up to the challenge, leading a group of businessmen to develop a new theater. They purchased a lot on Meeting Street from the Grand Lodge of Ancient Free Masons of South Carolina and organized The Charleston New Theatre as a joint-stock enterprise.

Using their business flair, they promoted the project as a civic improvement, engaged a prominent architect to design a world-class venue, and, during its construction, leased the property to William Abbott, an experienced actor-manager, who brought a company of players to town in anticipation of the launch.

They also managed a successful public relations campaign with the local press. On December 18, 1837, the *Charleston Courier* described the twelve-hundred-seat theater in detail: "Two full stories in height above a raised basement, the stuccoed brick building had a massive Ionic portico, with four columns, above an arcaded base. The portico was accessible only from within the building; entry from Meeting Street was through the arcade level. Three main doors opened to the lobby/vestibule, which had a ticket office at one side, ladies withdrawing room at the other, and a corridor leading to the boxes and seating floor. Above the richly ornamented auditorium was a large dome, at its center a forty-eight-lamp chandelier, eight feet across."

Left: Junius Booth Right: Edwin Booth *Library of Congress*

The theater attracted serious talent, including the "eminent Tragedian," Junius Booth, making his first appearance in Charleston in more than a decade. His characterization of Sir Giles Overreach was well received, with a reviewer in the *Southern Patriot* declaring it "among the finest exhibitions of histrionic power we have ever witnessed. . . . On the whole it was the most thrilling piece of acting we have ever seen. . . ." Another headliner was Fanny Elssler, the celebrated German ballerina, whose appearances in Baltimore and New York had caused riots among her fans outside the theaters.

After Abbott left Charleston in 1841, several managers ran the theater for the next twenty years. In 1858 and 1859, Edwin Booth played several engagements, reprising his father's roles as Richelieu, Hamlet, Giles Overreach, and Othello.

THE SOCIAL SCENE

In the winter months, plantation work was at a lull, so well-off Charlestonians organized their social lives around the time between Christmas and the Tuesday before Ash Wednesday. Besides art, sport, and theater, these activities included a busy round of musical concerts, subscription balls, and fine dining—as well as the "watering holes" found in hotels.

Hotels

Many of the hotels were not only resting places for travelers or tourists, but also gathering places for residents with the bonus of fine dining in most of them. Socializing in this way was a form of entertainment for many Charlestonians, and the proprietors knew that. Which is why a few hotspots in town kept the social scene alive.

MEETING AND QUEEN: ST. MARY'S HOTEL, THE PLANTER'S HOTEL, MANSION HOUSE HOTEL, MILLS HOUSE HOTEL

The property at Meeting and Queen Streets, owned by John Paul Grimke, was a double three-story brick house that accommodated both residential and commercial use, with tradesmen renting the cellar and other rooms.

Grimke's daughter, Mary, eventually inherited the house and outbuildings. When she married Henry Ward, he managed her estate and signed an agreement with hotel operator Francis St. Mary.

The hotel splashed on the scene on December 24, 1801, with a brief notice in the *South-Carolina Gazette*: "St. Mary's Hotel this day removed to that eligible situation and commodious house, the corner of Meeting and Queen streets, formerly occupied by Mrs. Miott, as a genteel boarding house. Gentlemen accommodated with boarding and lodging, or boarding alone. Breakfasts, dinners, etc. Soup every day—and suppers, beef steaks and oysters every evening, and in private rooms for select parties."

Within a year, Francis St. Mary relocated to the former Brockway's tavern on King Street, and Mrs. Miott moved her boardinghouse back to the location temporarily.

Less than a year later, on October 1, 1803, James Thompson—the former proprietor of the Carolina Coffee House—opened the Planter's Hotel in "that large airy and commodious building lately known as St. Mary's Hotel, to accommodate country gentlemen and their families with boarding and lodging. . . . His larder will always be furnished with the best the markets afford, and his liquors will be genuine and of the first quality."

In 1806, Mrs. Alexander Calder leased the property from Thompson and "spared no pains nor expense" to renovate for the "reception of the gentlemen planters from the country, as also for the citizens of Charleston, in a style that unites comfort, neatness, and convenience."

Within a few years, she and her husband also leased a boardinghouse on Sullivan's Island. At the same time, they moved the Planter's Hotel to the corner of Church and Queen Streets, at the location of today's Dock Street Theatre.

Mary Grimke Ward kept the location as income property until her death in 1822, bequeathing it and her other properties to her brother's children, the well-known abolitionists Angelina and Sarah Grimke. In 1825, they sold the house to Plowden Weston, whose Queen Street residence stood on the adjoining parcel. Weston's sons sold the Grimke house and lot to Otis Mills in 1836.

During the early 1840s, the location housed some of the offices of the US Courthouse, and from 1848 to 1852, the building was known as the Mansion House Hotel. In October 1852, the proprietor moved the Mansion House Hotel to Broad Street.

Meanwhile, Otis Mills acquired neighboring parcels on Meeting and Queen Streets, which brought his lot to a size large enough to build a substantial enterprise.

The Mills House Hotel was built at an estimated $200,000, a huge sum in 1853. The five-story hotel boasted an arched entryway and an iron balcony across the façade. Before it opened to the public, the *Charleston Courier* ran an article that highlighted the grand scale, modern amenities, and imports: stoves and furnaces from New York; ironwork, mantels, and chandeliers from Philadelphia; and furniture from Boston. Stone and marble work for the pavement and exterior steps were supplied locally.

According to the article, the hotel offered 180 guest rooms, a dining saloon, a separate gentlemen's dining room, and a ladies' "ordinary" on the second floor that had tables for 160. Each room had gas lighting, each floor included eight "bathing rooms" for ladies, with similar rooms for gentlemen on the first floor. Water for the baths, steam heating system, and in-house laundry was supplied by wells and cisterns on the property.

Mills House Hotel in 1865 *Wikimedia Commons*

The hotel would make a few more changes—and more headlines—in the coming years. (See Section 5: Doing the Charleston.)

CHURCH AND QUEEN: PLANTER'S HOTEL, CALDER INN

The Dock Street Theatre, which had been destroyed by fire some years previously, had been rebuilt into a townhouse sometime in the late eighteenth or early nineteenth century.

In 1809 Mr. and Mrs. Alexander Calder bought the townhouse, expanded it, and transformed it into the Planter's Hotel, which they relocated from the corner of Meeting and Queen.

The hotel, well-known for its hospitality, was an immediate success and became a favorite of visitors and residents alike. Wealthy planters and other elite guests frequented the Planter's Hotel, including the famous actor Junius Brutus Booth.

In 1816 the hotel's success required another renovation to include new guest rooms. In 1835 the iconic wrought-iron balcony and sandstone columns were added to the Church Street façade.

Adding to the hotel's success—if not creating it—were several legends and rumors.

One involved Junius Brutus Booth, who, while a guest there in 1838 for a performance at the Charleston New Theatre, is reported to have attempted to murder his manager, a man by the name of Flynn, in one of the hotel's guest rooms.

Another legend says the hotel was the birthplace of the famous Planter's Punch cocktail. The recipe itself mentions Jamaica, so it was likely brought to Charleston from there. In any case, it was made more famous through the Planter's Hotel.

The Calders eventually sold the hotel, and it changed hands several times before businessman J. W. Gamble purchased it in 1855 and renamed it the Calder Inn for its original owners.

The building would eventually return to its former use as a theater, though not for many years and only after the area had been altered by war, reconstruction, and a devastating earthquake.

Planter's Punch Recipe

Planter's Punch is a cocktail made of Jamaican rum, fresh lemon juice, and sugar cane juice. The September 1878 issue of the London magazine Fun *gave the recipe in a poem:*

> *A wine glass with lemon juice fill,*
> *Of sugar the same glass fill twice*
> *Then rub them together until*
> *The mixture looks smooth, soft, and nice.*
>
> *Of rum then three wine glasses add,*
> *And four of cold water please take. A*
> *Drink then you'll have that's not bad—*
> *At least, so they say in Jamaica.*

---

200 MEETING: THE CHARLESTON HOTEL

The Charleston Hotel at 200 Meeting Street was built on a lot that had been vacant after a fire in 1835. After construction started, it was struck once more by fire—the Great Fire of 1838—which destroyed the interior detailing. Rebuilding commenced, and it opened in 1839.

The Charleston Hotel in 1890 *Library of Congress*

The Charleston Hotel was an icon of Charleston's antebellum grandeur. Featuring a four-story Parthenon-style façade and a block-long colonnade with fourteen pillars, it boasted 170 bedrooms, bathrooms, reading rooms, reception rooms, parlors, two large dining rooms, and a shaving saloon.

Through the years, various other amenities were added that testified to its opulence, including elevators, hot and cold running water, a doctor and a pharmacist onsite, a poultry farm, a bakery, a telegraph office, a steam laundry, and its own electric plant.

The Charleston Hotel hosted several banquets, meetings, and balls, including those held by the South Carolina Jockey Club.

Among the visitors seeking the hotel's luxury and extravagance were Princess Louise, daughter of Queen Victoria; international soprano star Jenny Lind; Daniel Webster; Oscar Wilde; and three US presidents—Theodore Roosevelt, William Taft, and Calvin Coolidge.

Years later, after the Civil War had diminished the hotel's splendor to a boardinghouse with cut-rate rents, the local newspaper remembered the magnificence and grace of the Charleston Hotel's earlier years:

"Traveling men usually remember the places they visit by the kinds of hotels at which they stopped," wrote a *News and Courier* reporter in 1910. "In Charleston there is one hotel that the consensus of opinion has named 'The Best.' This is the Charleston Hotel . . . a part of [the city's] traditions."

Columnist Ashley Cooper (the pen name of *News & Courier* editor Frank B. Gilbreth Jr.) wrote in 1986 that the hotel was "one of the few remaining links with the romantic days of terrapin soup, gas lights and visiting royalty."

BALLS, COTILLIONS, AND BANQUETS

During the social season, which occurred during the winter—roughly Christmas through Shrove Tuesday—Charleston was ensconced in a variety of social activities, primarily the parties and dancing for which the city was renowned.

Charleston's balls, cotillions, and banquets each had distinct features that made each different, and though they were not all equally venerated, each played a part in the "season."

For instance, the balls held at Vauxhall Garden were informal as compared with other venues, as they were held in a garden arena, advertised in the newspaper, and charged admission. Regardless, they were still a vibrant part of the social scene.

Other balls were more exclusive and privileged. The debutante ball was one such event. A holdover from a seventeenth-century European custom in which aristocrats presented their daughters at court to find suitable husbands, the debutante ball was considered the quintessential rite of passage for young girls.

In eighteenth- and nineteenth-century South Carolina society, the debutante ball had evolved to be the primary event during the social season.

And while a debutante could be presented to society at any tea dance, party, or ball—some of the newspapers ran stories about several debutante balls held on the same night between November and January—it was considered more appropriate for the girl's "coming out" to be at an official ball held by organizations that were created specifically for that purpose.

Some of these organizations were men's groups, others were women-only groups, and yet others gave couples equal status. The criteria for membership in a debutante society were often shrouded in secrecy, but wealth was usually not a factor. Lineage and friendship were more important.

According to the strict etiquette of the time, a few details were the same regardless of venue: The debutante wore a white gown, was presented by her father or another male relative, and curtseyed before the members of society to whom she was being introduced. She then took her escort's arm and participated in the grand march, after which all debutantes took a collective bow, and the dancing began.

These lavish events were expensive, with great attention paid to every detail of the food, entertainment, and decorations.

ST. CECILIA SOCIETY

Charleston's St. Cecilia Ball has long been considered the "grande dame" of the ball organizations in the state.

Though organized as a musical society in 1766, the St. Cecilia Society had transformed into purely social events by 1822. The concert series was disbanded due to several factors. First, around 1815 musical interests began changing, which meant enthusiasm for the society's concerts declined. Then, two years later, the Charleston Theatre Company began a tour that disrupted the society's custom of sharing musicians with the local theaters. Finally, the Panic of 1819 affected the local economy, and the society was forced to cut back on its activities.

After the scant 1819–1820 season, the society dropped its concert series and for a few years presented a reduced number of dancing assemblies.

Though its concert patronage ended in 1820, the St. Cecilia Society refocused to hosting a yearly series of three or four elegant balls that only members and special guests could attend. Even as it became a public event, it remained the ultimate "insider status" for those in the Charleston area as well as in other parts of the country. Socialites came from as far away as Philadelphia and Boston to attend the most exclusive social event in the state.

The prerequisites for admission of new members were strict and complex, as were the rules for attendance at the ball. Reportedly, actors and actresses could not attend the ball, nor could divorced or remarried people.

A member's daughter could attend St. Cecilia parties only as long as she was unmarried and under the sponsorship of her father, unless she married a boy whose father, grandfather, or another ancestor was a member of the society. If the girl married a boy whose family was not a member, she would never again be eligible to attend the St. Cecilia party, nor would her daughters, in perpetuity.

Members could invite outsiders to the ball, but the guests were required to live at least fifty miles from Charleston.

Similar organizations appeared in other parts of the state in the late 1800s—notably the Assembly Ball and Cotillion in Columbia and the Assembly Ball in Greenville—and even smaller towns across the state began to have debutante balls as well, all modeled after the St. Cecilia Ball.

Though its purpose in finding husbands grew less serious through the years, the ball as an excuse to have a good time remained strong even into the twenty-first century.

The St. Cecilia Ball stopped only twice: for the Civil War and for World War II. During the Vietnam era, the debutante ball was overshadowed by political events, but it not only survived but also flourished afterward.

JOCKEY CLUB BALL

Horse racing at the Washington Course, offered by the South Carolina Jockey Club, was deemed the finest in the South. The club's annual races were held in January or February and were the high point of Charleston's social season.

So, it's no surprise that Race Week, held in February during the height of Charleston social season, was among the most elaborate and extravagant of all events in the area.

Race Week coincided with the gala social season of balls, parties, and dinners. The elegance and refined audience, so they said, rivaled the British course at Goodwood.

Funded by dues and investments, the Jockey Club hosted a dinner on Wednesday night and a ball on Friday night. Guests included non-members with proper social connections, which included local and out-of-town families. The St. Cecilia Ball and private balls in various mansions downtown rounded out the other evenings during Race Week.

The Jockey Club Ball was held every year at St. Andrew's Hall, commencing at 11:00 p.m. and closing at 6:00 a.m.

Race Week encompassed Charleston's entire social scene. Artist Charles Fraser wrote in 1843, "Schools were dismissed. The judges, not unwillingly, adjourned the Courts, for they were deserted by lawyers, suitors, and witnesses. Clergymen thought it no impropriety to sese [*sic*] a well contested race; and if grave physicians played truant, they were sure to be found in the crowd at the race ground. . . . The whole week was devoted to pleasure and the interchanges of conviviality; nor were the ladies unnoticed, for the Race Ball, given to them by the Jockey Club, was always the most splendid of the season."

Eliza Lee, Caterer Extraordinaire

After Sally Seymour's death in 1824, her daughter Eliza took over her cook shop at 78 Tradd Street. Over the years, she had learned all her mother's skills, so it was natural that she would take her mother's place at the city's premier caterer and culinary instructor.

She also married John Lee, a successful tailor whose business was close to the cook shop. Lee was a Black man and a member of the Brown Fellowship Society, the association of free African-American wealthy.

They purchased a home at 92 Tradd Street, a few doors down from her mother's cook shop, which they used as a boardinghouse, event space, and bakery. Eliza Seymour Lee became the go-to caterer in the city. The Society of the Cincinnati met regularly at her cook shop on Tradd Street well into the mid-1830s, as did the Charleston Hussars. She catered many of the private society meetings of Charleston's aristocracy, and she was the preferred caterer at the annual banquets for the South Carolina Jockey Club during Race Week.

John Lee soon gave up his tailoring business to become a caterer and boardinghouse proprietor. From 1840 through 1851, John and Eliza ran four establishments: The Mansion House on Broad Street (1840–1845), the Lee House (1845–1848), the Jones Hotel (1848–1850), and the Moultrie House on Sullivan's Island (1850–1851).

After John's death in 1851, Eliza continued to work as a culinary instructor until her death in 1874.

Although never proven, local legend says two of Lee's sons migrated north after the Civil War to become cooks. They began using Eliza's recipe for savory pickles and preserves, which eventually became so famous that it caught the attention of Henry Heinz, who bought the recipe and used it as the foundation for the Heinz 57 Sauce.

> It would seem that the entire animal and vegetable kingdoms had been placed at the command of the Club's caterer, that heaven itself had furnished the cooks.
> —A correspondent from the New York periodical, The Spirit of the Times, in Charleston for the Jockey Club Dinner that Eliza Seymour Lee catered.

Jockey Club Dinner Menu

BILL OF FARE

Turtle Soup
Fins and Steaks

FISH
Rock Fish, melted butter
Fresh Salmon
Black Drum, Worcestershire sauce
Broiled Shad

BROILED
Mutton, caper sauce
Turkey, oyster sauce
Capons, mushroom sauce
Vol au Vent Oysters
Westphalia Ham
Round of Beef
Smoked Tongue
Pig's Feet, with tomatoes
Fricasseed Terrapin

ROAST
Turkeys, brown gravy
Geese, cranberry sauce
Capons, gravy
Maccaroon Pies
Boned Turkey, in truffles
Beef, radish
Saddle of Lamb, mint sauce
Saddle of Mutton, gravy
Pigeon Pies
Vol au Vent of Sweet Bread

GAME
Venison, currant jelly
Wild Turkeys
Grouse
Pheasants
Quails

Pate de foi Gras
Chicken Salad
Canvas Back Ducks
Black Head Ducks
Teal Ducks
Snipe
Partridges
Pate de foi Doie
Lobster Salad

VEGETABLES
Green Peas
Asparagus
Parsnips
Carrots
Spinach
Rice
Bread
Potatoes

DESSERT
Plum Puddings
Lemon Puddings
Orange Puddings
Charlotte Russe
Blancmange
Jellies
Apple Tarts
Cranberry Tarts
Almond Cakes

ORNAMENT
Candied Fruits
Vanilla Ice Cream
Pineapple Ice Cream
Fruits, Nuts, Etc.

COFFEE

Supplying the Music for a Music-Loving City

In the early nineteenth century, German-born Johann Siegling went to Paris to learn musical instrument craftmanship before emigrating to Charleston. In 1819, he opened the Siegling Piano Ware House, later known as Siegling Music House, on King Street selling pianos, harps, and wind instruments.

During the antebellum times, production of American pianos was on the upswing, and business was good.

Charlestonians still maintained an active concert life, with the refined musical tastes of her high society preferring works in the European secular tradition, though sacred music had its devotees as well. This created a great demand for both classical and popular sheet music as well as the instruments.

To meet the demand, Siegling founded a music publishing house that produced the works and arrangements of local and European composers.

Years later, when the Civil War started, Siegling manufactured drums for the Confederate

Siegling Music Shop *Library of Congress*

army. After the war, his family took up the music business again. Siegling Music House remained a Charleston staple through 1970.

ST. ANDREW'S HALL AND SOUTH CAROLINA SOCIETY HALL

St. Andrew's Hall, a public building on Broad Street, served as headquarters for the St. Andrew's Society of Charleston as well as the venue for the social scene for upper-class Charlestonians. The hall was used for concerts, banquets, balls, and meetings

St. Andrew's Hall engraving, 1860 *Library of Congress*

for organizations, including the St. Cecilia Society and the South Carolina Jockey Club. The hall was also used for lodging, especially for significant guests such as President James Monroe in 1819 and General Marquis de Lafayette in 1825.

St. Andrew's Hall is distinguished as the location where delegates from South Carolina met on December 19, 1860, to discuss secession from the United States. The next day they met at Institute Hall on Meeting Street—later known as Secession Hall—and voted 169 to 0 to secede. (The South Carolina delegates ratified the Confederate Constitution at Secession Hall on April 3, 1861. South Carolina was the first state to secede from the Union.)

Both St. Andrew's Hall and Secession Hall were destroyed during a fire on December 11, 1861.

After the fire at St. Andrew's Hall, the South Carolina Society Hall on Meeting Street was used as a place for meetings and society events.

The South Carolina Society Hall was constructed in 1804 by the St. Andrews's Society for use as a school for orphans and indigents, as well as for social purposes.

The South Carolina Society Hall *Library of Congress*

In 1826 it became a secondary school with both a Male Academy and Female Academy, both of which closed in 1841.

Since then, the hall has been used as a dance school (specifically, cotillions), weddings, bar and bat mitzvahs, and business meetings—and in recent years, as a location for TV and movie shoots.

Entertaining a Soldier Pays Off

A few years of recreation and enjoyment may have saved the city during the Civil War.

William Tecumseh Sherman, the foster son of a prominent Whig politician in Ohio, graduated from the US Military Academy at West Point in 1840 and two years later was stationed at Fort Moultrie on Sullivan's Island, near Charleston.

Sherman had the opportunity to move within the upper circles of Charleston society, attending many of the parties and balls.

Like many of the young men who did tours at Fort Moultrie in the Antebellum Period, Sherman was impressed with Charleston. Years later, his biographers wrote about the time he spent there:

"Moultrieville, on Sullivan's Island quite near the fort, was at that time a place of fashionable resort during the summer season for the wealthy families of Charleston and South Carolina generally, many of whom had temporary residences there, to which they removed on the approach of hot weather to escape from the malarious influences of the city and lower country, and enjoy the cool breezes and the sea-bathing. Officers of the army were at that time sought after and hospitably entertained by nearly all of the better classes of society in the South, and Lieutenant Sherman was thus, upon his arrival at Fort Moultrie, ushered into a life entirely new to him. During the summer [of 1842] he made many agreeable and some valuable acquaintances, which were cemented and extended during the following winter when he, in common with the other officers, was almost overwhelmed with invitations to accept the hospitalities of the citizens of Charleston to whom they had been attentive at the fort."

In a letter to his brother back home, Sherman wrote of how much he enjoyed the high society of the Charleston upper class.

"I'll try and give you an idea of how our days pass in a garrison like this. Here at Fort Moultrie we have about 250 soldiers, divided into four companies. These are quartered some inside the wall, some outside. All the unmarried officers, eight of us, live inside; all the married, five, outside. This being the headquarters of the regiment, we have the Colonel and his band of about fifteen instruments.

"Every morning at daylight all get up at reveille, attend a drill, either as infantry or artillery, at sunrise; breakfast at seven, have a dress parade at eight, and half-an-hour after the new guard takes the place of the old one, a new officer relieving the old one. After that, each one kills time to suit himself, till reveille of next morning commences the new routine. Thus, it is every fair day except Sunday, when we have an extra quantity of music, parade, and inspection in honor of the day, and to keep our men in superfine order at church.

"Thus, you see that every day at nine o'clock and after, we [the off-duty officers] have nothing to do but amuse ourselves. Some read, some write, some loaf, and some go to the city [Charleston]. For the latter class, a barge is in attendance, going and coming. Although six miles from a city, we have all its advantages, whilst separated from its annoying noises, taxes, and expenses. . . ."

On his infamous March to the Sea (November 15 to December 21, 1864), he stopped within fifteen miles of Charleston, then turned and instead headed to Columbia, which he burned to the ground.

In a letter dated December 24, 1864, to General Henry Halleck, Chief of Staff of the US Army, December 24, 1864, Sherman noted that "communicating with the fleet in the neighborhood of Georgetown, I would turn upon Wilmington or Charleston accordingly to the importance of either. I rather prefer Wilmington, as a live place, over Charleston, which is dead and unimportant when its railroad communications are broken."

After the war, when Sherman visited Charleston, he mourned over his former home: "Anyone who is not satisfied with war should go and see Charleston, and he will pray louder and deeper than ever that the country may in the long future be spared any more war."

Finding a Way to Moultrieville

Beginning in the summer of 1792, James Hibben offered a daily ferry service, using rowboats, that connected the Charleston peninsula, Mount Pleasant village, and Sullivan's Island. With the transportation issue taken care of, over the next few years, the seasonal settlers formed a village at the southwestern end of the island called Moultrieville, which was incorporated in 1817.

This rowboat ferry service continued for several decades until it was replaced by a steamboat ferry in 1820. The state legislature empowered the town of Moultrieville to manage the ferry service in 1828, though other private ferry companies cropped up to compete.

RETURN OF AN OLD FRIEND

In 1824, at the age of sixty-seven, Marquis de Lafayette returned to the United States for a grand tour. The French Revolution had given way to the restoration of the monarchy in 1814, and in the United States, there were deep political divisions. On this trip, Lafayette hoped to restore the passion for liberty that had united his country in its own revolution.

He visited all twenty-four (at that time) states. One of the stops on his tour was Charleston, where he arrived on March 15, 1825, and was treated to three days of dinners, balls, and fireworks—and one important reunion.

Upon his arrival in South Carolina, Lafayette contacted Dr. Francis Huger—son of his old friend Major Benjamin Huger as well as his would-be prison rescuer (see Two Doctors and a Failed Prison Break, page 120)—and asked him to be his traveling companion.

Upon arriving in Charleston, he visited the Elms Plantation (now part of the Charleston Southern University campus), the Heyward-Washington House (now a museum), the William Gibbes House, and the Pinckney Mansion (formerly at 235 East Bay Street).

He also toured the Charleston Orphan House, City Hall, the Charleston Theatre on Broad Street, and St. Andrew's Hall on Broad Street.

The Huger family held a large reception for Lafayette at the Huger House at 34 Meeting Street. Lafayette insisted that Dr. Huger be equally held in honor during the festivities.

When Lafayette died in 1834, the US House and Senate chambers were draped in black. He has many tributes and memorials throughout the country, including a park directly across from the White House on Pennsylvania Avenue.

America has continued to pay homage to Lafayette through the years. In 1917, after the United States entered the First World War, Colonel Charles E. Stanton visited Lafayette's tomb in Paris and uttered the now famous words, "Lafayette, we are here." Every July 4, a joint Franco-American ceremony at the tomb honors this hero of the Revolutionary War. The American flag at his tomb has never been removed, even during the Nazi occupation in World War II.

In 2002, a Joint Resolution from Congress granted him US citizenship, one of only eight times in history this honor has been given.

Two Doctors and a Failed Prison Break

In 1794, after completing his medical studies in London, Dr. Francis Huger set out to tour Europe before returning to Charleston. During his tour he met Dr. Justus Erich Bollman, who had been instrumental in helping some of the French aristocracy escape the guillotine and resettle in England.

The two became friends and often discussed political issues, including Lafayette's incarceration. In his youth, Huger, the son of Major Benjamin Huger, had heard stories of when the great Lafayette had stayed at his plantation upon reaching America and the friendship between his father and Lafayette.

Huger and Bollman hatched a scheme to help Lafayette escape to America. They bribed a guard to pass letters to Lafayette. The letters seemed innocent; however, they wrote in the margins with lemon juice, communicating about the escape plan.

Portrait of Lafayette in Olmutz Prison
Library of Congress

Though laid out carefully, the plan ultimately failed. Lafayette would spend another five years in prison, and Huger and Bollman were captured and imprisoned as well. Huger and Bollman were given a light sentence—about eight months—and it is assumed that the judges were paid for such leniency.

The two men eventually returned to the United States. Bollman got caught up in Aaron Burr conspiracies and was arrested for treason. Meanwhile, Huger married the daughter of Thomas Pinckney and settled in Charleston.

LEISURE OF ANOTHER KIND

Like many towns and cities around the world, especially those with a busy port, Charleston had a reputation for being a bawdy and rowdy place on occasion—and those occasions were usually when ships from around the world docked in the harbor and let loose seamen into the streets.

Entrepreneurial types took advantage and provided the merchants and seamen entertainment in the form of taverns and brothels.

The city's first red light district was in what was then the waterfront area—now known as the French Quarter.

The Pink House at 17 Chalmers Street—in the center of the French Quarter—was constructed between 1694 and 1715 and was originally a tavern through the 1750s. At some point it came to be used as a brothel (and, in more recent years, an art gallery, a law office, and a residence). Because the building is still standing, the stories about the Pink House have become more entertaining over the years.

Just before the Revolutionary War, city officials, concerned that such activities with alcohol and prostitutes might interfere with protecting the city, pushed the red-light district a few blocks inland from the waterfront to an area known as Dutch Town (having been settled primarily by Germans). Relocation had little effect, and business continued, now on Fulton, Clifford, Magazine, West, Beaufain, Archdale, and Logan Streets, flanked by St. John's Lutheran and Unitarian churches.

By the 1850s, at the height of the Antebellum Period, most businesses in Charleston were thriving, and the bars and brothels were no exception.

Madam Grace Ups the Game

One notorious lady of the night was businesswoman enough to go professional—as much as one could in an industry that was illicit—saving up her own money to build her own brothel.

Not much is known about Grace Piexotto's early life other than that she was born in the late 1700s. What is known is that she was smart enough to save up her money

The Big Brick building *Point North Images*

and bold enough to bribe officials for building permits to build her own establishment from the ground up.

Completed in 1852, The Big Brick, so named because it was constructed with large red bricks, was the only building in Charleston planned and constructed specifically for use as a brothel. The building had salons where the men could smoke cigars, drink brandy, and read newspapers, and the upper floors were divided into small rooms with single beds to afford her clientele some privacy.

Grace trained "her girls" in manners, style, and the art of conversation, all to suit her southern gentlemen clients. The police and civil leaders looked the other way—possibly because they may have been frequent customers—and Madam Grace became wealthy and respected by the gentlemen whose secrets she kept. According to local legend, Margaret Mitchell used her as the model for the fictional character Belle Watling in her book, Gone with the Wind.

Madam Grace welcomed anyone to her establishment, provided they could pay, of course. One year, she sent a letter to the faculty at the College of Charleston asking them to keep their students away, as they were not able to afford The Big Brick's rates.

When Grace died in 1880, none of the churches in the area wanted to take responsibility for burying the most notorious madam in the South. Finally, the Unitarian

Church agreed to pay for her services—but unfortunately, no one came. Her girls had to work—consoling the men, presumably—and none of the gentlemen could afford to be seen attending her funeral.

However, according to local custom, it was proper to send an empty carriage to a funeral if one could not attend. And so, many of the men sent theirs. This is how Grace Piexotto ended up having the second longest funeral procession in the history of Charleston. (The longest was for John C. Calhoun, who had served as seventh vice president of the United States.)

SEE FOR YOURSELF: ANTEBELLUM PERIOD

When you're in town, be sure to see where history was made during the Antebellum Period with these tours.

Walking Tour of White Point Garden

The southern tip of the Charleston peninsula was originally known as Oyster Point—because of the oyster shells at the edge of the water—but by the 1700s was known as White Point.

White Point Garden—also known as Battery Park (the Battery, or seawall, rings the park on two sides)—was a military post at one point, but from the mid-1800s on, it was a well-known public recreation site. The 6.5-acre park provides views of Fort Sumter, Castle Pinckney, Patriots Point, the Charleston Light on Sullivan's Island, and Charleston Harbor, where legend has it "the Ashley and Cooper rivers meet to form the Atlantic Ocean."

The patch of greenspace is equally known for its historical monuments as it is for being an ideal place for a shaded stroll or a picnic on the grounds. Oak trees and palmettos provide ample shade, and, as a tribute to its former name, the walking path is covered with crushed oyster shells.

The park is bordered by King Street (at the end of which is the Fort Sumter Hotel), Murray Boulevard (along the Battery), East Battery Street (which becomes East Bay Street within a few blocks), and South Battery Street.

The high seawall and promenade along East Battery is known as High Battery, whereas the part of the Battery along Murray Boulevard is known as Low Battery.

The park has a storied military past. It was occupied by Fort Broughton during the Revolutionary War. Broughton's Battery, a large brick fort with forty-five cannons, was located at the end of Church Street in 1737. It was dismantled in 1784, and the property was subdivided and sold. Several private residences are now on this site.

The White Point Bandstand *Point North Images*

In the War of 1812, Fort Wilkins occupied the site, with cannons lining the waterfront borders to protect the city from invasion. The cannons have since been moved inside the park. (One of them is actually a fake, placed there as a joke.)

During the Civil War, the park was the site of military action again. As Charleston was being evacuated, tons of munitions were set off in the empty space to ensure no weapons would fall into Union hands.

Several memorials, historical markers, and military relics are scattered throughout White Point Garden, including: a French cannon from the Revolutionary War found in Camden, South Carolina; a rapid-fire gun from a Spanish ship during the Spanish-American War; an eleven-inch cannon from the USS *Keokuk* that fired shells at Fort Sumter in 1863; two Confederate columbiads (large cannons) used in the defense of Fort Sumter; a seven-inch Brooke rifle (large cannon) found at Fort Johnson; four thirteen-inch Union mortars weighing seventeen thousand pounds each; and a 1918 World War I howitzer.

One notable memorial is a marker commemorating the hanging of the "Gentleman Pirate" Stede Bonnet. He and his crew were hanged in 1718 and, in keeping with tradition for pirates, buried below the low water mark in the marshes off White Point Garden.

The park contains a statue of Sergeant William Jasper, who retrieved the "Moultrie flag" (Second SC Regimental flag) after the mast was shot in two at Fort Sullivan (now called Fort Moultrie) during the battle of Sullivan's Island on June 28, 1776. He attached the flag to an artillery sponge and mounted it on the parapet of the fort. Jasper reportedly told Colonel Moultrie, "Colonel, don't let us fight without our flag." (The quote is on the monument near the base.)

The bandstand in the center of the park was completed in 1907. The bandstand once hosted regular concerts, but complaints about noise and commercial activity from neighbors caused the city to outlaw concerts there in 1978. Renovated in 1985 and again in 2010, it is now used for weddings and other limited events.

Admission to the park is free, and free curbside parking is available along the Low Battery on Murray Boulevard.

Walking Tour of Dock Street Theatre, South Carolina Society Hall, Charleston Library Society

This tour takes you to a few of the places that were popular during the Antebellum Period, when Charleston was at her most elegant and the pursuits of entertainment, leisure, and education were paramount.

Start on Church Street at the Dock Street Theatre.

DOCK STREET THEATRE

135 Church St., Charleston, 29401

The name may be confusing, but the street was actually called Dock Street at one point. This is the site of the first building in the country constructed specifically for theatrical performances. The original building was destroyed in a fire, and the later structures have gone through renovations and upgrades over the years. It has been a theater, a boardinghouse, a hotel, and today is a theater again. (For more info on the Dock Street Theatre, see pages 17, 106, and 182.)

Go to Queen Street and turn left. Go a block to Meeting Street and turn left. Cross Broad Street. The South Carolina Society Hall will be within the first block on the left.

SOUTH CAROLINA SOCIETY HALL

72 Meeting St., Charleston, 29401

The Society Hall was constructed in 1804 by the St. Andrew's Society for use both as a school and for social purposes. After St. Andrew's Society Hall was destroyed in

Dock Street Theatre *Point North Images*

the Civil War, it became a meeting place for that group as well. Over the years, the hall has been used as a dance school, a ballroom, and a venue for weddings, bar and bat mitzvahs, and business meetings. (For more info on the South Carolina Society Hall, see page 114.)

Go farther down Meeting Street until you come to Tradd Street and turn right. Go a block to King Street and turn right. Continue on King Street, crossing Broad and Queen Streets. Within the first block after Queen Street, the Charleston Library Society will be on the right.

CHARLESTON LIBRARY SOCIETY
164 King St., Charleston, 29401
Initially called the Charles Town Library Society and later the Charleston Library Society, the library was formed in 1748 as a private subscription library to support education and the arts and sciences. By 1755, they had incorporated. The books and materials were stored at various locations until, through the generosity of the South Carolina Jockey Club, the organization was able to find its permanent home at this location.

The society was responsible for the creation of the College of Charleston, the first municipal college in the country created in 1770, and the Charleston Museum, created in 1773. (For more info on the Charleston Library Society, see pages 138 and 175.)

At this point, you are about three blocks from your starting point at the Dock Street Theatre. To return there, go to Queen Street and turn left. Cross Meeting Street and go another block to Church Street. The theater will be on the right.

SECTION 4:
THE LATE UNPLEASANTNESS

Civil War and Reconstruction, 1861–1902

I'm going to Charleston, back where I belong. . . .
I want to see if somewhere there isn't something left
in life of charm and grace.
—RHETT BUTLER IN *GONE WITH THE WIND*

Timeline Highlights: 1861–1902		
Elsewhere		**Charleston**
1861: Kinematoscope (forerunner to the motion picture camera) patented by Coleman Sellers.	1861–1869	1861: Civil War begins with shots fired by Confederates onto Union-held Fort Sumter.
1861: Dickens publishes *Great Expectations*.		1863: The 587-day Federal bombardment of Charleston begins on August 22.
1861: Queen Victoria issues a proclamation of neutrality, which effectively recognizes the Confederate States of America.		1863: Half of Charleston Library Society's materials sent to Columbia for safekeeping.
1861: George Eliot (Mary Ann Evans) publishes *Silas Marner*.		1863: The Union assault on Battery Wagner is led by the 54th Massachusetts all-Black unit (portrayed in the 1989 film *Glory*).
1862: Hugo publishes *Les Miserables*.		1864: CSS *H.L. Hunley* rams the USS *Housatonic* and becomes the first submarine to sink a vessel in war.
1863: Eighteen countries meet in Geneva and agree to form the International Red Cross.		1865: Union troops occupy the city.
1864: Twelve nations sign what will be known as the Geneva Convention.		1865: Sherman comes within a few miles of Charleston but turns to Columbia instead.
1864: Tolstoy publishes *War and Peace*.		1865: First Memorial Day held at old Washington Race Course.
1865: Lee surrenders to Grant at Appomattox.		1865: Nat Fuller hosts Reconciliation Dinner.
1865: Ratification of the Thirteenth Amendment, which bans slavery.		1865: Avery Normal Institute (later the Avery Research Center for African American History and Culture at the College of Charleston) founded.
1865: Lewis Carroll publishes *Alice's Adventures in Wonderland*.		1865: Street railways begin operating in Charleston.
1866: Monet paints *Camille*.		

Elsewhere		Charleston
1870: US Congress creates Department of Justice. 1870: Jules Verne publishes *Twenty Thousand Leagues Under the Sea.* 1871: Queen Victoria opens Royal Albert Hall. 1872: Metropolitan Museum of Art opens in New York. 1873: Color photographs first developed. 1873: Panic of 1873 stock market crash. 1875: Mark Twain publishes *The Adventures of Tom Sawyer.* 1876: A. G. Bell is granted a patent for an invention known as the "telephone." 1876: First tennis tournament in America. 1876: First transcontinental railroad (Transcontinental Express) travels from New York to San Francisco in eighty-three hours and thirty-nine minutes. 1876: Edison receives a patent for the mimeograph. 1877: Edison receives a patent for the phonograph.	1870	1870: Magnolia Gardens opens for tourists. 1870: Savannah and Charleston Railroad reopens. 1874: Charleston Library Society merges resources with Charleston Apprentice Library Society. 1875: Jockey Club reorganizes. 1877: President Hayes orders federal troops to leave Charleston. 1879: US Custom House built.
1880: John Philip Sousa becomes leader of US Marine Band. 1880: Gilbert and Sullivan produce *The Pirates of Penzance.*	1880	1881: Charleston City Square renamed Washington Square Park. 1882: Dr. Manigault purchases a building on behalf of the Carolina Art Association to be used as an art school.

Elsewhere		Charleston
1881: Clara Barton establishes American Red Cross.		1881: Charleston City Square renamed Washington Square Park.
1881: Gunfight at O.K. Corral in Tombstone, Arizona.		1882: Dr. Manigault purchases a building on behalf of the Carolina Art Association to be used as an art school.
1882: R. L. Stevenson publishes *Treasure Island*.		
1882: Edison flips switch to first commercial electric power plant, lighting one square mile of lower Manhattan.		1882: Last Jockey Club races.
1883: Brooklyn Bridge opens to traffic.		1883: Charleston Driving Association begins harness and flat racing on Wagener's farm.
1884: Proclamation of eight-hour workday in America.		1886: Earthquake measuring 7.0 hits Charleston, causing widespread destruction.
1884: Washington Monument is completed.		
1885: Mark Twain publishes *Adventures of Huckleberry Finn*.		1887: First Gala Week held to showcase Charleston's post-earthquake recovery efforts.
1885: Statue of Liberty arrives in New York.		1888: Only tea plantation in America begins production.
1886: First ticker-tape parade in New York during dedication of Statue of Liberty.		
1887: First Groundhog Day in Punxsutawney, Pennsylvania.		
1889: Eiffel Tower officially opens at Exposition Universelle.		
1889: First jukebox in operation at Palais Royale Saloon in San Francisco.		

Elsewhere		Charleston
1891: The Music Hall in New York (later Carnegie Hall) has grand opening. 1891: Edison patents the motion picture camera. 1892: Ellis Island opens to begin processing immigrants. 1893: New Zealand becomes the first country in which women can vote in a national election. 1894: Coca-Cola bottled and sold for the first time. 1898: USS *Maine* explodes and sinks in Havana, which leads to US war with Spain.	1890	1890: First Rockville Regatta held. 1891: Rev. Daniel Jenkins opens the Jenkins Orphanage and hires musicians to teach the orphans to play. 1897: Public amusement resort begins construction on Isle of Palms. 1899: Jockey Club disbands and donates its assets to the Charleston Library Society.
1901: Pan-American Exposition is held in Buffalo, New York. 1901: First Nobel Prizes are awarded. 1902: Carnegie Institution for Science is founded. 1902: Willis Carrier creates the first air conditioner.	1900–1902	1900: Charleston Exposition Company forms to solicit funds for an expo. 1901–1902: South Carolina Inter-State and West Indian Exposition held on the grounds of the former Washington Race Course.

TRAJECTORY OF WAR: SECESSION PARTIES, BALLS-ON-A-SHOESTRING, AND MEMORIALS

These were dark days for the South in general and Charleston in particular. "War is hell"—a quote attributed to Sherman in the later years of the war—is true no matter the location or circumstances, but it quickly became a reality in Charleston.

Nevertheless, Charlestonians found a way to keep up their spirits with any amusements they could find.

After South Carolina seceded from the Union (the first state to do so), delegates reassembled in St. Andrew's Hall amid a flurry of exhilaration and revelry. The enthusiasm carried them through the early days of the war.

On April 12, 1861, at 3:30 a.m., Louis DeSaussure, a physician and planter, invited guests to gather on the roof and piazzas of his house on East Battery to toast and cheer "the fireworks" of the start of the Civil War.

For most people, the war was business—and pleasure—as usual.

SECESSION HALL, CHARLESTON, SCENE OF THE PASSAGE OF THE ORDINANCE OF SECESSION. FROM A PHOTOGRAPH.

Secession Hall *Library of Congress*

St. Andrew's Hall Secession Party *Library of Congress*

As the war dragged on for years—and was not favorable to the South—Charlestonians tried to keep some of their traditions alive, and they found ways to adapt.

Their approach to fashion was a microcosm of adaptability. During the war, they continued to hold balls, and the women wore their best gowns, but because of the dangers of skirmishes, the attendees would stay the night. The next day, the women wore the same dresses, but outfitted it with a "second-day bodice" so they would appear different.

Their attitudes might seem like denial, but in fact they were a degree of fortitude. The residents would need it. By the end of the war and throughout Reconstruction, Charleston was broken. Many entertainment activities were suspended, though the residents fought to have them resume as soon as possible.

The First Memorial Day

The war eventually took its toll on the lives and the spirits of the city's residents. The South Carolina Jockey Club's Washington Race Course was taken over by Confederate soldiers and used as a prisoner-of-war camp.

Washington Race Course, 1865 *Library of Congress*

Nearly 260 Union soldiers had died in the camp and were buried together behind the judges' stand. After Union forces occupied the city, the bodies were exhumed and reinterred with respectful markers. They were exhumed again in 1871 for proper military burial at the national cemeteries in Beaufort and Florence, South Carolina.

On May 1, 1865, approximately ten thousand emancipated slaves and Unionists gathered at the Washington Race Course to honor the Union soldiers who died there. The ceremony marked the first Memorial Day and included speeches, a picnic, and a parade.

APPEALING TO TASTES: ART, BOOKS, AND FOOD

By the end of the Civil War and into the Reconstruction period, Charleston struggled to regain her high culture and society. In the postwar years, people had little money for theater and music, and many of the venues had been destroyed by bombs or fire.

Some semblance of the cultured life remained, though. Just enough to remind Charlestonians that they were people of taste.

Carolina Art Association and The Gibbes Art Gallery

The Carolina Art Association was dormant during and after the Civil War, but activity picked up again by 1878 and art shows again became a favorite leisure pursuit.

In 1882, association president Dr. Gabriel Manigault purchased a building on Chalmers Street for an art school. Initial interest was high: In the first two years,

Gibbes Museum postcard *Wikimedia Commons*

it enrolled five hundred students. Unfortunately, economic conditions had not yet smoothed out, and the school was forced to close in 1892 due to lack of funds.

An unexpected boon helped the struggling association: James S. Gibbes, a loyal patron of the arts, bequeathed $100,000 to the Carolina Art Association for a building to be used as a hall for the exhibition of paintings, rooms for students in the arts, and for general promotion of the arts.

By 1905, the organization had changed its name to the Gibbes Art Gallery (later the Gibbes Museum of Art).

Charleston Library Society

In 1863 the society's librarian sent half of the library's collections to Columbia for safekeeping. Sadly, all items sent to Columbia were destroyed in the 1865 fires.

The society spent the next decade rebuilding its collection, which was helped by merging resources in 1874 with the Charleston Apprentice Library Society (founded in 1824).

By 1899 the collection had grown so large that the librarian implemented the Cutter classification system along with a card catalogue, which replaced the old printed-and-bound catalogues.

The following year, the Jockey Club of South Carolina disbanded and transferred its property to the society. The society sold the Washington Race Course, which enabled the organization to create an endowment specifically to purchase books. Two years later, the society accepted its first institutional member, the College of Charleston.

The Jockey Club's generosity provided a means of revenue that continues to benefit the organization today.

The Academy of Music

Though music and theater were in lull during this time, they were not completely abandoned. One of the few remaining performing arts venues was also one of the best.

The four-story building at 225–227 King Street originally was occupied by Kerrison's Department Store, built in 1830. The building was destroyed by the Great Fire of 1838, then rebuilt and operated by Kerrison's until 1852. Another mercantile firm, Browning & Leman, took it over until it was sold to New Yorker John Chadwick.

Chadwick remodeled it as a twelve-hundred-seat theater, modeled after the European opera houses and designed with excellent acoustics. During construction Chadwick called it the Charleston Opera House and described it as "superior to any theatre in New York, save Booth's Theatre and the Grand Opera House." By the time it was opened in 1869, the name was changed to Academy of Music.

In 1875, comedian John Owens bought it and renamed it Owens Academy of Music. The 1886 earthquake left the venue severely damaged, and without insurance, Owens lost the property.

It was later acquired by Albert Sottile's Pastime Amusement Company, renamed the Riviera Theatre, and converted into a motion picture theater. See Section 5: Doing the Charleston for more on the Riviera's place in Charleston history.

Cuisine

The war did not diminish Charleston's reputation for excellent cuisine. There was simply less food for a while. But the city could make do.

THE HORS D'OEUVRE CAPITAL

Rather than set aside one of the city's greatest enjoyments, Charlestonians rose to the occasion and got creative. Which is how Charleston became known as the hors d'oeuvre capital of America.

After the war, most Charlestonians did not have the means to provide the grandiose meals that were served in previous years. But they still wanted to entertain, so they started serving cocktails with dine-and-dash hors d'oeuvres. Napkins (always linen and sometimes monogrammed) were used instead of plates, and guests helped themselves.

KEEPING THE SEYMOUR LEGACY ALIVE

Sally Seymour and her daughter, Eliza Seymour Lee, both mentored many of Charleston's chefs. They in turn taught culinary skills to others, keeping the legendary Charleston cuisine alive through generations. Here are a few of the more prominent African-American chefs.

Nat Fuller (1812–1866) apprenticed under the great cooks in Charleston, including Eliza Seymour Lee, and grew to be one of the most sought-after caterers in the area.

For many years, Charleston cuisine was French, which takes great skill to master, after which the saucier commands much respect. Fuller was widely known for a variety of sauces including catsups, caper, lemon, Madeira, mayonnaise, mushroom, mustard, olive, oyster, tomato, white sauce, and Worcestershire. He was also a master mixologist and was famous for his Brandy Smash, gin with bitters, and Mint Julep.

Fuller was called a "culinary genius" and was a prolific caterer. He gained his freedom, became the caterer of choice after Eliza Seymour Lee retired, and owned his own restaurant, The Bachelor's Retreat, in the late 1800s. In 1865, he hosted an interracial reconciliation dinner celebrating emancipation and the end of the Civil War.

Nat Fuller's reconciliation dinner was reenacted on April 19, 2014, to commemorate the 150th anniversary of the original feast. A cocktail reception was held at 103 Church Street, the location of The Bachelor's Retreat (now The Charleston Renaissance Gallery) with dinner in the long room at McCrady's Restaurant.

Thomas Tully (1828–1883) was born into freedom on Edisto Island. He apprenticed under Fuller and became a master at pastry and confections. He later partnered with free Black pastry chef, Martha Vanderhorst.

Fuller also trained William G. Barron (1847–1900), who was born into slavery. He opened his own restaurant and catering facility in 1882.

As a teenager, James F. Perrineau (1868–1953) worked as a cook for Irish baker and confectioner, John E. Heffron. He catered for the St. Andrew's Society, the St. Cecilia Society, the South Carolina Society, the Hibernian Society, and would periodically cook for the Medical Society. He later opened a restaurant at 391½ King Street.

PLANTATIONS AND PARKS

Plantations as Tourist Attractions

In the late 1800s, the plantations started to become tourist attractions, including those that had suffered huge devastation during the war. Even the ruins were a popular draw.

One tourist described a boat excursion of the Ashley River in a letter to the editor of the *Charleston Courier* on April 25, 1872. Here are a few excerpts:

"Messrs Editors: — Seeing the advertisement of the steamer *Pocosin* for an excursion up the Ashley River on Saturday the 20th instant, we determined to throw aside, temporarily, the pursuits of business, and abandon ourselves to such pleasures and pastimes as this might afford . . .

" . . . A little further on, a sight less cheerful greets out vision, and recalls some saddening reflections—an hundred homeless chimneys are peering through the beautiful trees on all sides, like gaunt spectres of the past, burned and whitened and scarred . . .

"Without event other than the occasional excitement of shooting at several 'gators,' to the extreme delight of the little children and the shootists; and the total nonchalance and quiet contempt of the alligators, we finally reached our destination—'Middleton Place.'

"The princely mansion, with endless wealth of picture galleries, numbering among its stores some of the most beautiful and valuable pieces of art in the world, and its library of choicest literature, now stands a pile of smouldering ruins, whose very stones cry out, 'Let us have peace'; but the beautiful (though neglected) terrace, the trees, the japonicas, the flowers, the crystal spring, the lawn, the winding walks, the inviting shade, the changing sunlight, subdued by the floating clouds, the placid river beyond, the warbling birds, the soft, fresh, fragrant air, renders it still a charming place, and makes you forget yourself and feel as though transported to another sphere.

"A few hours enjoyed here, we re-embarked and . . . the steamer hauls up to a steep and picturesque bluff, and after a little maneuvering and some tall walking over a very narrow plank, we are again on terra firma, at 'Drayton Hall,' the country seat of the Rev. Mr. Jno. Drayton. Here a picture awaits our view that pen or brush is futile to describe. Here, in the very midst of the original forest, beneath the fostering shade of the lofty tulip, the poplar, the cedar and the ancient oak, is a perfect

Magnolia Steamer, 1900 *Library of Congress*

Archdale Hall on Ashley River, 1865 *Courtesy of South Caroliniana Library, University of South Carolina, SC*

wilderness, (thirty acres) of the most gorgeous azaleas the eye ever rested on; the various kinds and colors combined by the artistic hand of its owner . . .

"Our greatest regret is that so few comparatively of our citizens avail themselves of these delightful excursions. . . ."

Only two plantations—Drayton Hall and Archdale Hall—survived the war, though Drayton Hall had been in disrepair before the war, and Archdale Hall was destroyed by the earthquake of 1886. Drayton Hall was renovated, and some of the other plantation homes were rebuilt. The famous Middleton Gardens were restored. They remain popular tourist spots today.

Washington Square Park

This park sits alongside a block of Meeting Street, from the intersection of Meeting and Broad Streets and the intersection of Meeting and Chalmers Streets, and is bordered by wrought iron gates and palmetto trees. Washington Square Park is one of the first public parks in Charleston. A portion of the park's 1.48 acres originally housed "Corbett's Thatched Tavern" before the area was repurposed in 1818 as a public gathering space and official city square.

WASHINGTON SQUARE, SHOWING W. L. I. PITT AND TIMROD MONUMENTS, CITY HALL, AND ST. MICHAEL'S CHURCH, CHARLESTON, S.C.

Washington Square Park postcard *Courtesy of South Caroliniana Library, University of South Carolina, SC*

It was called Charleston City Square until 1881, when it was renamed in honor of the first American president. Its new title was painted over the entrance gates to mark the occasion.

Several statues and monuments are in the park, including a memorial that pays tribute to the Washington Light Infantry: a forty-two-foot-tall granite structure, which is a miniature version of the Washington Monument in Washington, DC.

White Point Garden

At the start of the Civil War, Battery Park became a fortification for the city, complete with cannons to defend the city.

After the war, the bathing house was torn down, the area was redeveloped into a garden, and the name was changed to White Point Garden.

It became a repository of relics and memorabilia, with a predominant military theme. Some of the guns from Fort Sumter were relocated there, along with guns from the USS *Keokuk*, which was sunk (and later salvaged) by Confederate troops in 1863. Other artillery pieces and cannons from the Revolutionary War made their way to the garden.

The only non-military item was the bandstand in the center, where concerts were held.

East Battery, 1909 *Library of Congress*

Country's First Tea Plantation

In the late 1700s, tea bushes (*camellia sinensis*), first arrived in the United States from China. Over the next 150 years, several planters made attempts to propagate and produce tea for consumption, but none were successful.

Finally in 1888, Dr. Charles Shepard founded the Pinehurst Tea Plantation in Summerville, north of Charleston, where he produced award-winning American-grown teas.

Dr. Shepard continued to grow tea on his plantation until his death in 1915. After his passing, the plantation closed, and his tea plants grew wild for the next forty-five years. The plants were later transplanted to the Charleston Tea Plantation, originally a 127-acre potato farm, on Wadmalaw Island, south of Charleston. The tea plantation changed hands twice more—to William Barclay Hall and then to Bigelow Tea Company—and the name was changed in June 2020 to Charleston Tea Garden. To date it remains the only commercial tea plantation/garden in America.

FORMATION OF JENKINS ORPHANAGE BAND

During Reconstruction, while many in the city strove to bring back the cultured life they'd lost, others were in even more dire straits, with lost homes and families. These were the Black orphans of the war, freed by proclamation but now enslaved to poverty and homelessness.

Despite their desperation, they too would find their way to entertainment, though it would take a few years and the saving grace of the Reverend Daniel Jenkins to get there.

One day in December 1891, Reverend Jenkins came across four homeless Black boys huddled together in a freight car. A former slave and orphan himself, he knew there were no facilities in the city that could care for them.

He took the situation to the City of Charleston and was allotted a yearly stipend of $1,000 for an orphanage. At that time, it was the only facility for Black orphans in the state. Originally located next to the old jail downtown, Jenkins Orphanage received dozens of neglected children almost as soon as it opened its doors. It soon filled to capacity.

The city's stipend was not enough to cover expenses, so he had to find other means to sustain the orphanage. He sent out requests for old musical instruments, and asked the Citadel, the local military college, for its old uniforms. With those donations in hand, he recruited two musicians to teach the children to play music.

The good reverend didn't do it for the love of music. In fact, he couldn't play any instrument. His motivation was money to keep the orphanage running.

The idea was almost certainly inspired by the success Booker T. Washington—the South's most famous Black educator at the time—had achieved using choral performances to gain publicity and donations for the Tuskegee Institute.

Reverend Jenkins also believed that teaching the children to play instruments gave them valuable skills, along with their other lessons in baking, butchering, farming, and printing.

The children trained several hours a day in addition to completing their other chores and lessons. They were quick learners. In just two years, the Jenkins Orphanage Band began touring the United States and abroad.

Jenkins Orphanage exterior, 1937 *Library of Congress*

Though it was formed to help support the orphans' home, the Jenkins Orphanage Band would become the training ground for dozens of top musicians and would influence the development of jazz. (See more about the band's rise to fame over the years in Section 5: Doing the Charleston.)

THE SPORTING LIFE

After the war, sports continued to be an important part of leisure and entertainment in Charleston. It took a few years to get back into the rhythm of sports, but it did happen, albeit in different or limited forms.

The Jockey Club's Attempted Revival and Eventual Demise

Horse racing was in decline after the Civil War. During the war, the Washington Race Course was used as a prison for Union soldiers, and many valuable racehorses were lost during the war, used as cavalry horses.

The loss of thoroughbreds during the war, coupled with the resulting economic decline, left the South Carolina Jockey Club in disarray and effectively killed horse racing in the state.

But no one could say the South Carolina Jockey Club didn't fight the good fight.

The club reorganized in 1875. It printed a revised rulebook, and in 1876, more than one hundred members paid dues. It was a start—or, rather, re-start.

At that point, the club had two tangible assets: real estate and a cache of Madeira wine that had survived the Civil War, hidden on the grounds of the South Carolina Asylum in Columbia. When the club sold the wine in 1877, the club was able to refurbish the Washington Race Course and start a new horse racing season.

It was a valiant effort. The February 1878 races were spread over four non-consecutive days, two of them Saturdays. Attendance was low, but Charleston had become a regular stop on the flat-racing circuit. When entries came in from several states in 1879, hope sprang eternal, and the Jockey Club added a winter meet. The new tramlines helped connect downtown with the race course.

But then hope began to wane. Breeding thoroughbreds had become a luxury beyond the means of most area planters. This meant fewer entries, coupled with a series of cold and wet Februarys. Race Week ceased to be the social "be-all" that it once was. All that combined caused attendance to slack off, which meant lower ticket receipts.

At this point, the Jockey Club members realized they could not continue. Racing took place for the last time in February 1882. Though Jockey Club–sanctioned thoroughbred horse racing had stopped in Charleston, a new racetrack north of the Washington Race Course filled the entertainment gap in 1883. The Charleston Driving Association's half-mile course on F. W. Wagener's farm showcased harness and flat racing into the early twentieth century.

In 1884, the race course grounds were leased as farm and pastureland.

Over the next few years, the club tried to revive the sport but failed. On December 28, 1899, the club disbanded, and its assets were donated to the Charleston Library Society.

The racetrack was part of the land used for the S.C. Inter-State and West Indian Exposition, held between 1901 and 1902. Horses raced on the track during the expo. After the City of Charleston purchased the property from the South Carolina Library Society, the Washington Race Course became Hampton Park.

Washington Race Course Lives on at Belmont

One piece of Charleston's early horse racing history still exists.

In 1901 the grounds of the former Washington Race Course were used for the South Carolina Inter-State and West Indian Exposition. It was there that August Belmont Jr., a wealthy New York banker, noticed the four stone pillars at the entrance to the expo. He asked to buy them, but instead the City of Charleston offered them as a gift.

The brick posts were shipped to New York, repaired, and reinstalled at the new Belmont Park on Long Island, New York. On May 4, 1905—Belmont's opening day— nearly forty thousand people streamed through the South Carolina Jockey Club gates.

Today, Charleston's Washington Race Course stone pillars still mark the entrance of Belmont Park, home of the Triple Crown Belmont Stakes.

Rockville Regatta

Beginning in the 1800s, Rockville was a summer escape for many of the planters in the area. The small town, located at the end of Wadmalaw Island (west of Charleston), offered creeks and rivers and cool breezes under a canopy of live oaks.

The river beckoned—and residents with sailboats answered. In 1890, two cousins challenged each other to a sailing contest, and the Rockville Regatta was born. For the broken and defeated Charlestonians, still navigating the loss of the war and Reconstruction, the competition was a respite from harsh reality.

In the first regatta, cousins Isaac Jenkins Mikell and John F. Sosnowski challenged each other to a sailing contest. Mikell put up the *Mermaid* against Sosnowski's *Undine*.

The details of the first regatta are lost to history (and legend), but the regatta—the oldest (though not the largest) in the state—became a favorite pastime of Charlestonians, and it continues today. Held annually the first weekend in August, the Rockville Regatta typically attracts about forty-five entries. The Sea Island Yacht Club in Rockville was rebuilt as a public works project during the Depression.

Post-Earthquake Celebrations

An earthquake struck Charleston at 9:50 p.m. on August 31, 1886. It caused sixty deaths and damage to two thousand buildings totaling about $6 million ($158.42 million in today's calculations). By all accounts, it was one of the most powerful and damaging earthquakes to hit the East Coast of the United States.

Scientists have classified it with an estimated magnitude of 6.9–7.3. Most of the buildings in the city sustained damage, and many had to be rebuilt. Structural damage was reported from as far away as Alabama, Kentucky, Ohio, Virginia, and West Virginia.

As soon as the city was cleaned up, it was time for—what else?—a party. With the same fortitude—and dedication to entertainment—that she had shown through the years, Charleston bounced back with entertainment.

To encourage tourism, the city's leaders planned a week-long celebration to show off how well Charleston had recovered from "the greatest earthquake east of the Mississippi." The gala was held the first week of November 1887, a little more than a year after the earthquake.

The first gala was so successful that the city held one every year after that, with each larger and more festive than the last.

The November 4, 1889, edition of the *Macon Telegraph* described the upcoming Gala Week:

"The city itself will be a pretty fair 'show' during the week with the multitude along the streets, the flags and arches and the long array of tastefully ornamented windows, brilliant illuminations by night and the thronging crowds by day and night. It would be well worth a visit to see the gay scene and take part in it even if there were nothing more than this. The official programme tells the story of the week. It includes fireworks by day and night, boat races and ship races, sham battles on the lake, military drills, parades and contests, trades displays and torchlight processions, fantastic and otherwise, floral exhibitions, steamboat excursions up the rivers and around the finest harbor on the coast, baseball and balloon ascension. On the last night, Friday, the harbor will be illuminated and war times will be recalled by representations of vessels running the blockade and the bombardment of Fort Sumter."

The Great Charleston Cyclone of October 1893 finally halted the yearly event. Recovery from that storm pushed Gala Week to the next spring, but the fete wasn't the same. The gala eventually faded into memory, but it had accomplished its purpose of displaying Charleston as a town that loves to celebrate.

SOUTH CAROLINA.— THE RESURRECTION FESTIVAL OF CHARLESTON—A SCENE ON KING STREET DURING JUBILEE WEEK.
FROM A PHOTO.—SEE PAGE 796.

Charleston Resurrection Festival *Courtesy of South Caroliniana Library, University of South Carolina, SC*

PLAYGROUND OF THE SOUTH

Charleston's reputation as an entertainment magnet was solidified in 1897 when Dr. J. S. Lawrence built a public amusement resort on the Isle of Palms, just north of the city.

The island had originally been called Hunting Island, then Long Island, and after development, Dr. Lawrence renamed it Isle of Palms in part because of the palm trees and in part to attract tourists. Before long, the island had earned the nicknames "Playground of the South" or "Coney Island of the South."

An article in the July 26, 1898, edition of the *Charleston Courier* marked the occasion: "A great event for the city, the Seashore Road formally opened yesterday. When the *Commodore Perry* left the new dock of the Charleston Seashore and Railway Company at 9 o'clock yesterday afternoon her spacious deck was crowded with people, all anxious to be among the first to visit that, as yet, unknown country, stretching vaguely behind the familiar shores of Mount Pleasant and Sullivan's Island. *The Sappho*, her deck also crowded with people, and the *Pocosin*, not so well patronized, steamed out of their docks just a moment before."

Initially the island had no lodging, so visitors gathered at the pavilion for a day trip of fun. The pavilion included a restaurant that served meals for 50 cents, a merry-go-round, and "hop night" dances on Tuesdays and Fridays. The pavilion also featured a Ferris wheel that was the largest in the world at that time. On a clear day, the Ferris wheel was visible from the Battery on the peninsula, over fifteen miles away. The ride was built for the Chicago World's Fair in 1892 and used by the Cotton Congress in Atlanta and Coney Island in New York before coming to the Isle of Palms.

Later, a type of rollercoaster called "the steeple chase" was imported from Coney Island. The ride had five mechanical horses that allowed riders to race around a U-shaped course. The winner received the next ride free.

The island was accessible only by ferry before a bridge was built in 1929. A plantation-style bell rang out "last call" at 11:30 p.m., and everyone rushed to meet the last ferry headed to Charleston for the night.

A fifty-room hotel was built in 1906, at which point the Isle of Palms became its own destination point for visitors.

Isle of Palms postcards *Courtesy of South Caroliniana Library, University of South Carolina, SC*

Sullivan's Island: Another Playground Nearby

In the middle 1800s, trolleys—first horse-drawn and later electric—were introduced to the peninsula and within a decade, the streetcars had made their way to Sullivan's Island as well. With both ferry and streetcar services available, tourists were drawn to the island, which prompted more facilities to accommodate them.

Private investors stepped up in 1884 and built a first-class resort called the New Brighton Hotel, situated beyond Moultrieville near the center of the island. The resort also featured three beach cottages in addition to the hotel. At first the resort was profitable, but after a massive hurricane in 1885 and the earthquake of 1886 devastated the local economy, the New Brighton closed.

In was later sold at auction, and when the economy rebounded, the New Brighton Hotel reopened in 1895 as the more modest Atlantic Beach Hotel.

SOUTH CAROLINA INTERSTATE AND WEST INDIAN EXPOSITION

By the start of the next century, Charleston had recovered sufficiently from the Civil War and Reconstruction to regain her confidence with a whirlwind of entertaining. First up was the South Carolina Interstate and West Indian Exposition.

Commonly called the Charleston Exposition or the West Indian Exposition, the idea of a regional trade exposition was floated in the late 1890s with a goal of strengthening weak trade with Latin America and the Caribbean. With harbor traffic on the decline since the Civil War, the expo's proponents aimed to position Charleston as the key port of exchange, thereby stimulating the local economy. The Charleston Exposition Company was formed in 1900 to solicit funds.

Initially, the federal government offered no support—it finally gave formal approval just before the start of the expo—and there were no official exhibits from foreign governments. The South Carolina General Assembly finally allocated $50,000, but there was lukewarm support from the business community. The Charleston Exposition Company managed to raise other funds through private and corporate subscriptions to stock, a municipal bond issue, and donations of convict labor.

When further funds were not forthcoming—and Charleston's high society deemed it too self-promotional—local businessman Frederick Wagener donated 250 acres of his property on the Ashley River for use for the exposition. Additional property was leased to the company by the Charleston Library Society, who had obtained the deed to the Washington Race Course after the South Carolina Jockey Club disbanded in 1899.

The company hired New York architect Bradford Gilbert to design the exposition. Gilbert had been the supervising architect of the Cotton States Exposition and had designed New York's first skyscraper. He chose a Spanish Renaissance style, with the buildings an off-white color, which led to the venue's nickname, "The Ivory City."

The grounds were divided into areas for Nature and Art, with principal buildings labeled Administration, Agriculture, Art, Auditorium, Commerce, Cotton Palace, Fisheries, Machinery, Mines and Forestry, Negro, Transportation, and

Scenes from the Charleston Exposition, 1902 *Library of Congress*

Women's. The grounds featured the Sunken Gardens and held a variety of statuary, among them six original historical groups, that were placed in the Court of Palaces.

The primary focus was the Cotton Palace, a 320-foot-long building with a seventy-five-foot-tall dome. Other key buildings included the Palace of Commerce and the Palace of Agriculture.

The midway was much like a county fair, with an Eskimo village, carnival thrill rides, a house of horrors, and a four-hundred-foot-long painting of the Battle of Manassas. One of the most popular attractions was a miniature railroad displayed by the Miniature Railway Company. There were, of course, souvenirs for sale, such as commemorative medals and pins.

Twenty states participated in the expo. State buildings included Illinois, Maryland, Missouri, New York, and Pennsylvania (which featured the Liberty Bell in its exhibit); Cincinnati and Philadelphia had city buildings; and special exhibits highlighted Cuba, Puerto Rico, and Guatemala.

The expo was held from December 1, 1901, to June 20, 1902. Many notable dignitaries attended, including President Theodore Roosevelt.

Thomas Edison also visited the expo in April 1902 and brought along his new camera for a panoramic view of the Charleston Exposition. He placed the camera in the center of the expo grounds near the exhibit buildings. The cameraman photographed and panned his camera simultaneously. The film, now part of the Library of Congress Digital Collection, shows "the walkways, pools of water, bridges over

the pools, exhibit buildings, bandstands, statuary, and decorations of all nature that, put together, made up the Exposition in Charleston in 1902."

The expo was challenging on several fronts. Besides the lackluster funding, the weather was poor, some exhibits opened late, and the president pushed back his visit from February to April.

Financially, it was a complete bust. Attendance was disappointing—only 674,086 showed up—and receipts totaled $313,000 against a cost of $1,250,000.

And yet, all was not lost. In true Charleston fashion, disappointment was remade into something new.

After the exposition, the City of Charleston paid the Charleston Library Society $32,500 for the eastern portion of the land—seventy acres high ground and twenty acres marsh—which included the old race course. The grounds contained the expo's formal court, main buildings, and the bandstand. The area was renovated and renamed Hampton Park.

In the 1910s the state acquired the western portion of the expo grounds that ran along the Ashley River and built the new campus of the Citadel.

Lowndes Grove, which was the Women's Building in the exposition, remains and is used today as an event facility.

SEE FOR YOURSELF: CIVIL WAR AND RECONSTRUCTION PERIOD

When you're in town, be sure to see where history was made during the Civil War and Reconstruction period with these tours.

Civil War Battle Sites

Charleston is famous for, among other things, being the place where the Civil War started. Both the defense of the city and the attempts to overtake it were hotly contested battles—and some of those sites still exist. Here are a few. They are not located on the Charleston peninsula, so a road trip—and in the case of Fort Sumter, a boat trip—will be required to visit.

(Note: Some of these require admission fees, some have guided tours, and occasionally some include war reenactments.)

FORT SUMTER AND FORT MOULTRIE
340 Concord St., Charleston
1214 Middle St., Sullivan's Island
https://www.nps.gov/fosu/index.htm
Fort Sumter and Fort Moultrie sit at the entrance to Charleston Harbor. Both are operated by the National Park Service.

Fort Sumter, site of the first shot of the war, is in the middle of the harbor and accessible only by boat. Boat tours leave from the Fort Sumter Visitor Education Center at Liberty Square at 340 Concord St. (near the South Carolina Aquarium). Entrance to the building is free; the boat trip to Fort Sumter has a fee. Exhibits interpret the historic elements of the site, and park rangers provide talks.

Fort Moultrie, though it faces the harbor, is located at 1214 Middle St. on Sullivan's Island, which is across the Cooper River and beyond Mount Pleasant. Entrance to the park is free. Self-guided brochures are available onsite and a twenty-two-minute orientation film is offered every half-hour. Fort Moultrie is also the burial site of Osceola, the famed Seminole warrior.

McLeod Plantation

SITE OF CAMP FOR 54TH MASSACHUSETTS COMPANY

325 Country Club Dr., Charleston, 29412
https://ccprc.com/1447/McLeod-Plantation-Historic-Site
McLeod Plantation, located on James Island (just south of Charleston), is a thirty-seven-acre plantation established in the 1850s. The grounds include a riverside outdoor pavilion, a corridor of oaks, and the McLeod Oak, estimated to be six hundred years old.

Today the historic site is managed by the Charleston County Parks and admission includes interpretive tours of the main home, grounds, and nearby slave homes; information about the Gullah/Geechee heritage; and details of the spirituality of the people who lived on the plantation.

The plantation's strategic importance during the Civil War is its role in housing the free-Black Massachusetts 54th Infantry Regiment prior to its assault on Battery Wagner (as depicted in the movie Glory).

FORT LAMAR

Fort Lamar Road, Charleston, 29412
https://scgreatoutdoors.com/park-fortlamarhp.html
An important part of the Confederate defense, Fort Lamar is the site of the June 6, 1862, Battle of Secessionville. It was initially called Tower Battery because of its seventy-five-foot observation tower, but it was renamed for Colonel Thomas Lamar, who commanded the Confederate troops at the battle who held off the Union army that outnumbered them three-to-one. Near the fort is a mass unmarked grave of 341 Union soldiers.

A short self-guided tour/hiking trail takes you past some of the historic sites and gives a scenic view of the marsh.

Reenactments of the Battle of Secessionville are held every year, weather and other public health concerns permitting. The fort is free and open during daylight hours.

CSS *HUNLEY* MUSEUM

1250 Supply St., Charleston, 29405
https://www.hunley.org/

On the night of February 17, 1864, the Confederate submarine *H.L. Hunley* sank the Union sloop USS *Housatonic* near Charleston Harbor. The submarine sank in Charleston Harbor, killing all eight crewmen. The fate of *Hunley* was a mystery for more than a century until the wreck was found in 1995 and raised in 2000.

A replica of the submarine sits in front of the Charleston Museum, but the actual vessel is at the Warren Lasch Conservation Center.

During the week, the center is an active laboratory for preserving the *Hunley*. On weekends, visitors can tour the facility and learn about discoveries the wreckage has yielded through interactive exhibits and activities.

SECTION 5:
DOING THE CHARLESTON

The Charleston Renaissance, 1903–1940s

Come quickly, have found heaven.

—ALFRED HUTTY, AN ARTIST CONSIDERED
ONE OF THE LEADING FIGURES IN THE
CHARLESTON RENAISSANCE, TO HIS WIFE
UPON VISITING CHARLESTON

Timeline Highlights: 1903–1940s

Elsewhere		Charleston
1903: First Tour de France bicycle race held. 1904: London Symphony Orchestra gives first concert. 1905: Picasso begins his "pink period." 1908: London hosts Olympic games.	1903–1909	1905: Gibbes Museum opens to the public. 1905: Jenkins Orphanage Band plays for President T. Roosevelt's inauguration. 1906: Hampton Park created. 1909: Ashley Hall School established. 1909: Jenkins Orphanage Band plays for President Taft's inauguration.
1910: The "weekend" becomes popular in the United States. 1910: Ocean Liner SS *France* (known as "Versailles of the Atlantic") launched. 1911: First Monte Carlo rally.	1910	1910: Peoples Office Building constructed. 1913: Charleston Library Society building constructed.
1921: BBC is founded. 1921: Unknown Soldier interred at Arlington National Cemetery. 1922: T. S. Eliot founds *The Criterion*. 1924: World Chess League founded at The Hague. 1925: Gertrude Stein publishes *The Making of Americans*. 1925: F. Scott Fitzgerald publishes *The Great Gatsby*.	1920	1920: Nation's First Preservation Society founded. 1925: Publication of Heyward's novel, *Porgy*. 1927: Gloria Theatre opens. 1929: Grace Memorial Bridge opens across the Cooper River.

Elsewhere		Charleston
1930: Sir Thomas Beecham founds the London Philharmonic Orchestra. 1936: Dale Carnegie publishes *How to Win Friends and Influence People*. 1936: Jesse Owens wins four gold medals in Berlin. 1937: Amelia Earhart is lost on a Pacific flight. 1939: World War II begins.	1930	1931: Preservation Ordinance enacted throughout the city. 1931: Footlight Players theater group established. 1934: Gershwin arrives to collaborate with Heyward on *Porgy and Bess* opera. 1937: Dock Street Theatre reopens.
1940: Hemingway publishes *For Whom the Bell Tolls*. 1941: Japanese attack on Pearl Harbor. 1941: *Citizen Kane* is released. 1945: George Orwell publishes *Animal Farm*.	1940	1947: Historical Charleston Foundation established.

RENAISSANCE ARTISTRY

As she made her way out of the depths of Reconstruction, Charleston gained a boost from the arts community, as a wave of writers, musicians, artists, and actors flocked to the city to initiate what would come to be known as the Charleston Renaissance. It carried the city through the Great Depression.

Societies and Organizations of the Arts

A great many organizations dedicated to art and culture cropped up at this time, among them the Charleston Sketch Club at the Gibbes Museum, the Charleston Etchers' Club, the Poetry Society of South Carolina, the Society for the Preservation of Old Buildings, the Society for the Preservation of Spirituals, and the Garden Club of Charleston.

CHARLESTON'S ART SET

The Charleston Renaissance is the period between World Wars I and II, when Charleston experienced a surge in the arts. The Charleston Renaissance, as part of the larger artistic movement known as the Southern Renaissance, helped stimulate the tourist industry in Charleston. As the architects, artists, historical preservationists, and writers in Charleston expressed their art, they helped improve the city.

Smith and Verner were Charleston natives, Taylor was from the upstate of South Carolina, and Hutty's home was New York.

The oil paintings, prints, and watercolors of the Charleston Renaissance artists documented life in Charleston and the surrounding area. The prints, including woodblocks and etchings, were sold to tourists and other visitors, which helped spread the imagery of Charleston throughout the country.

VISUAL ARTS

Alfred Hutty

Wintering in Charleston on Tradd Street and summering in Woodstock, New York, Alfred Hutty had a great setup during the Charleston Renaissance, just doors away from Elizabeth O'Neill Verner, Anna Heyward Taylor, Alice Ravenel Huger Smith, and DuBose Heyward.

He served in World War I as an artist working to camouflage ships. After the war, he visited Charleston and immediately cabled his wife: "Come quickly. Have found heaven."

He split his time between Charleston and Woodstock and is considered a founder of the Woodstock Art Colony. In Woodstock, he had established himself as a painter of impressionist landscapes in oil and watercolor. After moving to Charleston, he took up etching and drypoint and became known for his detailed prints of local street scenes, historical buildings, farm life, landscapes, and African-American residents. His prints won several awards and medals.

Hutty was active in several arts organizations, including the Society of American Etchers, the Allied Artists of America, the National Arts Club, and the American Watercolor Society. He helped found the Charleston Etchers' Club. He was the first American artist elected to the British Society of the Graphic Arts.

Hutty taught at the Carolina Art Association, whose gallery would later become the Gibbes Museum of Art. He was the first professional director of the then-new Carolina Art Association Art School.

Hutty exhibited his work nationally at the American Watercolor Society, the Art Institute of Chicago, and the National Academy of Design. The Gibbes Museum of Art has the single largest collection of his work. Some of his other works are displayed at the Cleveland Museum of Art, the Greenville (SC) County Museum of Art, the Los Angeles County Museum of Art, the Metropolitan Museum of Art, the South Carolina State Museum in Columbia, and other museums and libraries.

Alice Ravenel Huger Smith

Though she received basic training at the Carolina Art Association early on, Alice Ravenel Huger Smith was mostly self-taught in her craft.

She began her art career as a portraitist, copying old family images and painting for friends and family. She tried out woodblock printing and etching and eventually settled on watercolor as her preferred medium. She later taught etching, with Elizabeth O'Neill Verner one of her more notable pupils.

Smith was involved in the artistic community in Charleston and was a founding member of the Charleston Etcher's Club and the Southern States Art League. She was also active in the Carolina Art Association, the Historic Charleston Foundation, and the Music and Poetry Society.

She preferred rural landscapes to Charleston's urban scenes for her subjects, and she was interested in portraying vanishing ways of life. She illustrated a volume by her father, historian D. E. H. Smith, entitled *The Dwelling Houses of Charleston*. Published in 1917, the book sparked the historical preservation movement in the city.

Philip Simmons

An American artisan and blacksmith specializing in the craft of ironwork, Philip Simmons focused on decorative ironwork as a blacksmith for seventy-eight years. Between those years, the craft went from shaping practical objects such as horseshoes to an art form.

As a child, Simmons visited the workshops of craftspeople in his neighborhood. He became especially interested in a smithy on Charlotte Street that was operated by Peter Simmons (no relation to Philip), a former slave. When he was thirteen, Philip Simmons quit school to apprentice with Peter Simmons and became a full blacksmith at eighteen years old.

Philip Simmons created objects to supplement his income, including tools, fireplace pokers, and a cup holder for a Volvo that was crafted from a coat hanger. Most of his work was created at his workshop at his home on Blake Street.

He began working with ornamental and decorative ironwork in 1938 at his own blacksmith shop. A few years later, Simmons received a commission from Charleston businessman Jack Krawcheck, who commissioned a wrought iron gate for the rear of his store on King Street.

New iron was unavailable because of the demands of the war, so Simmons had to create the gate out of scrap iron. Over the next seven decades, Simmons created about six hundred separate pieces, including fences, gates, iron balconies, and window grills. He forged and designed iron gates all around the city of Charleston and throughout the rest of the Lowcountry. His pieces have gone as far afield as France and China. He has ironwork at the South Carolina State Museum and a special "star and fish gate" created for the Smithsonian Institution, in which the fish appear to be swimming.

Simmons retired at age seventy-five but continued to teach his craft to younger artisans for the rest of his life.

In 1982, the National Endowment for the Arts honored him with a National Heritage Fellowship, which is the US government's highest honor in the folk and traditional arts.

In 1994, he was inducted into the South Carolina Hall of Fame.

In 1998, Governor David Beasley gave him the Order of the Palmetto, the state's highest honor.

In 2001, he was awarded the Elizabeth O'Neill Verner Governor's Award for "Lifetime Achievement in the Arts." He was also honored by the South Carolina Legislature for his work.

In 2006, he received an honorary doctorate from South Carolina State University for his contributions to the field of metalworking.

Anna Heyward Taylor

After graduating from South Carolina College for Women in 1897, Anna Heyward Taylor traveled to Holland in 1903 to study with the painter William Merritt Chase before traveling around Europe, China, and Japan for another few years. She served in the American Red Cross in France and Germany during World War I, the first woman from South Carolina to serve with the Red Cross in France during the war.

After returning to America, Taylor went to Radcliffe College for graduate work and spent summers studying printmaking at a Provincetown print workshop. She became an expert in white-line woodblock printing, a technique that makes it possible for an artist to print multiple colors from the same block rather than requiring a separate block for each color. Later Taylor painted in both oils and watercolor, but still preferred printmaking.

After additional study and travel, Taylor moved to New York City in 1920 and remained there until the end of the decade, when she returned to Charleston. She opened a studio on Atlantic Street, where several other leaders of the Charleston Renaissance also had studios.

She became known for her prints illustrating life in the Charleston area, including agricultural subjects, local fauna and flora, architecture, street scenes, and the city's tradespeople.

Elizabeth O'Neill Verner

Often referred to as "the best-known woman artist of South Carolina of the twentieth century," Elizabeth O'Neill Verner was active in several art organizations and founded and/or served on boards for the Charleston Sketch Club, the Charleston Etchers' Club, and the Southern States Art League.

A graduate of Ursuline Academy in Columbia, she attended the Pennsylvania Academy of Fine Arts and studied under Thomas Anshutz. After she returned to Charleston, she married E. Pettigrew Verner.

Verner did not become a professional artist until after her husband's death in 1925, at which point she was the sole supporter for her family. Like some of her contemporaries, she published her prints in books that could be sold to tourists. She also sought commissions and began specializing in drawings of historic buildings to further the cause of preservation. Among her clients were Harvard Medical School, Princeton University, the United States Military Academy, the University of South Carolina, and the Williamsburg Historic District.

Verner worked at a studio within her residence at 38 Tradd Street. She made drawings, drypoints, etchings, and pastels of Charleston—mainly buildings, landscapes, and street scenes. She worked occasionally as a book illustrator, notably DuBose Heyward's novel *Porgy*.

LITERATURE

John Bennett

As a child, John Bennett learned to draw and became skilled at silhouettes. He dropped out of high school to work for a newspaper, later working as a freelance author and illustrator.

Bennett was self-educated as an illustrator and wanted to go to art school, but he was not able to afford it until the mid-1890s. While he saved the money, he wrote a children's book about a boy in Elizabethan England who is kidnapped into a company of actors. *Master Skylark* was first serialized in *St. Nicholas Magazine* and later issued in book form. It became a bestseller. Today it is considered a classic and has never been out of print.

To combat recurring health problems, his doctor advised him to recuperate in a warm climate. In 1898 he moved to Charleston, where he had friends, and married Susan Smythe, the daughter of a prominent Charleston family.

He became active in promoting culture in the city and incorporated Black folktales and the Gullah language into his lectures and stories.

In 1920, he worked with other Charleston Renaissance figures to found the Poetry Society of South Carolina, which sponsored visits by many distinguished poets of that time.

A few years later, Bennett published three more books that grew out of his interest in folk tales, including *Madame Margot: A Grotesque Legend of Old Charleston*, *The Doctor to the Dead: Grotesque Legends and Folk Tales of Old Charleston*, and the most successful, *The Pigtail of Ah Lee Ben Loo*, a collection of international folk tales, which was a runner-up for the Newbery Award and for which he created two hundred vibrant silhouettes as illustrations.

Josephine Pinckney

Being a direct descendant of Eliza Lucas Pinckney and Governor Thomas Pinckney as well as the daughter of one of South Carolina's last great rice planters were the least of the attributes that made Josephine Pinckney famous.

She graduated from Ashley Hall School, where she helped establish a literary magazine, and attended the College of Charleston, Radcliffe College, and Columbia University. She received honorary degrees and memberships in sororities as well as many honors for her writing, including the Southern Authors Award.

Pinckney played a key role in the literary revival that engulfed the South after the first World War. One of the founders of the Poetry Society of South Carolina, she emerged over the next decade as a poet of national reputation when her work appeared in journals such as the *Saturday Review of Literature and Poetry*, as well as in numerous anthologies.

Pinckney was involved in other institutions and activities of the Charleston Renaissance, including the Carolina Art Association, the Charleston Museum, the Dock Street Theatre, and the many undertakings of the historic preservation movement.

She was active in the Society for the Preservation of Spirituals from its inception in 1922, helping with the transcriptions and musical annotations for the African-American songs included in *The Carolina Lowcountry*.

In the 1930s, she turned her writing talents to prose, publishing short stories and later best-selling novels. Her editor at Viking Press recalled the "charm and grace of her character, the intelligence of her insights into people, the delights of her Charleston ambiance tempered by her cosmopolitan ways and her irony."

Though she traveled often, she maintained her home in Charleston and the family plantation on the Santee River, El Dorado.

PRESERVATION

Laura Bragg

Born and educated in Massachusetts, Laura Bragg received a degree in library science from Simmons College in 1906, then came to Charleston in 1909 to serve as librarian of the Charleston Museum (at that point located on Rutledge Avenue). Within a few months, she was elected president of the Charleston Natural History Society.

Fiercely devoted to public education, she initiated what became known as "Bragg Boxes," which brought the museum to people who were unable to visit. The wooden boxes with hinged panels opened to show dioramas of local natural history or cultural history. They were accompanied by teaching materials, most developed by Bragg, and objects the students could handle. She created more than five dozen Bragg Boxes over the years.

Starting about 1913, the Bragg Boxes were circulating exhibits that went out to students, first in Charleston and later into Charleston County and the state. The boxes were available to both white and Black schools—which were segregated at the time—even though many Black schools could not afford their use until 1927 when they received donations.

Other museums, including the American Museum of Natural History in New York, incorporated Bragg Boxes in their own educational outreach programs.

Bragg was promoted to curator of books and public instruction in 1915 and developed the museum's first educational programs. In 1920, she was named director of the Charleston Museum, the first woman in the country to hold such a position.

Her directorship brought her into close contact with the artists and writers of what would later be known as the Charleston Renaissance. In the 1920s she was one of the founders of the Poetry Society of South Carolina, the Southern States Art League, and the Southern Museum Conference.

She added a children's library and reading room that loaned books, which became Charleston's first public library, which was initially housed in the Charleston Museum.

She didn't shy away from controversy. Rather, she embraced the opportunity to change and improve the lives of all people. In 1921, she opened the museum to Black visitors on Saturday afternoons, less than four years after the museum's own trustees had put in place a policy denying admission to Black people.

She connected the Charleston Museum with the wider American museum field through the American Alliance of Museums (AAM) meetings, which she hosted in Charleston in 1923 and became a board member in 1924. She directed the museum's purchase of the historic Heyward-Washington House in 1929, which opened to the public in 1930 as the city's first house museum.

She returned to Massachusetts in 1931 to serve as director of the Berkshire Museum, but when she retired in 1939, she returned to Charleston.

Susan Pringle Frost

With a family lineage dating back to the eighteenth century, Susan Pringle Frost seemed destined to a life of leisure following a privileged childhood and two years at a prominent boarding school.

However, the decline of the Frost and Pringle rice plantations on the Santee River along with the failure of her father's fertilizer business redirected her life and her energies. She learned basic stenographic skills and entered the workplace, initially as a secretary to architect Bradford Lee Gilbert, designer of the South Carolina

Inter-State and West Indian Exposition of 1901–1902 and later as court stenographer for the US District Court.

Her experience served her well. In 1908, she began investing in real estate and purchased several dilapidated historic properties in the city and converted them into profitable holdings.

She also became active in the national movement to advance women's rights, and in 1914, she was elected the first president of the Charleston Equal Suffrage League (later renamed the League of Women Voters).

In 1918, after sixteen years of stenographic work, she resigned from the federal court and opened an office on Broad Street devoted to expanding her successful real estate business. Among her more famous real estate transformations was the rehabilitation of the section of East Bay Street that later became famous as Rainbow Row.

She took her experience with rehabilitating old buildings in Charleston and shared her concerns for preserving the city's history with other like-minded citizens. In 1920, she organized the Society for the Preservation of the Old Dwelling Houses of Charleston (later shortened to the Preservation Society of Charleston). Under her leadership, the organization cultivated what became known as "historic preservation" not only in Charleston but in other cities as well.

The Society's success in raising local awareness of preservation led to the city's 1931 ordinance to create the nation's first "historic district."

Frost served as zoning monitor on the Board of Adjustment through the 1940s. Her initiatives in historic preservation contributed directly to improvements in Charleston and helped make it a national tourist destination.

Albert Simons

With a sixty-year career as an architect and preservationist, Albert Simons played a key role in the Charleston Renaissance.

After degrees at the College of Charleston and University of Pennsylvania, Simons traveled through Europe studying architecture and creating hundreds of travel sketches and watercolors. He returned to Charleston in 1915 and became one of the first instructors at the Clemson School of Architecture.

In 1920, he joined with Samuel Lapham VI to create the architectural firm Simons & Lapham, which focused on a variety of projects, including public, transportation, and building restoration. The firm did well during the Great Depression, thanks to commissions from the federally funded Works Progress Administration.

Over the years, Simons received much acclaim for his work in architectural design, preservation, and city planning. His firm worked with the City of Charleston to protect and restore historic homes and was involved with the Historic American Buildings Survey. Among the firm's more famous work are the restoration of the now-famous Rainbow Row and the re-conversion of the Planter's Hotel into the Dock Street Theatre.

Simons helped create the first historic district in America and the first Board of Architectural Review (BAR). He was a founding member and played a key role in the Society for Preservation of Old Dwellings, today known as the Preservation Society of Charleston.

Simons also served on the boards of many of the city's civic and cultural institutions, including the College of Charleston, the Charleston Museum, the Charleston Library Society, and the Poetry Society of Charleston.

As a professor at the College of Charleston for more than twenty years, he started the School of the Arts, whose building is named after him, and created the first art history course at the college.

Ferdinanda Legare Waring

Following the death of William Legare, his older sister Ferdinanda inherited a portion of Old Towne Plantation, including the house. At the time, the house was in disrepair and the grounds were a mass of weeds and overgrown vines.

By the late 1930s, she bought the other portions owned by family members and began a major redesign project that would become her life's ambition.

Along with restoring and expanding the house—now known as the Legare Waring House—she installed the formal live-oak avenue leading up to the house and planted thousands of azaleas and camellias on the property. Employees from her flower business and egg farm helped her cultivate the informal gardens surrounding the house. Their work resulted in eighty acres of picturesque gardens, including the freshwater lagoons near the house.

In the 1970s, she sold the property to the state for use as a public park. Her vision and stewardship helped protect the property and revive it into the public trust, Charles Towne Landing State Historic Site (see more information about Charles Towne Landing in Section 1: See for Yourself).

When she sold the property to the state, she said: "We don't own any land and we don't own any house. God has given it to us in trust, to make into something better during our lifetime."

The Charleston Library Society

From 1835 until moving to its current location on King Street in 1914, the Charleston Library Society occupied the Bank of South Carolina building at the corner of Church and Broad Streets. That building was paid for with "Brick" memberships, which were permanent memberships for one-time lump sums. Several of these memberships are still in use today, generations later, by Charleston families.

In 1914, the society constructed its building at 164 King Street, the first place to call its own where it could house its collection. It was in this new building that members John Bennett, DuBose Heyward, Josephine Pinckney, Beatrice Witte Ravenel, Albert Simons, and many others studied, read, and wrote.

Much of the works of these artists maintained the cultural foundation of twentieth-century Charleston.

The Charleston Library Society's collection includes rare books, pamphlets, manuscripts, and the records of the society—those that weren't lost in Columbia during the Civil War.

The society also maintains a collection of newspaper files, considered the world's largest and most complete collection of eighteenth- and nineteenth-century Charleston newspapers. Society members have free access to the collections and its circulating library; non-members have access with a daily research fee.

In 1996, the society expanded its facilities into an adjacent building, which contains a children's reading room, audio and video collections, and offices.

Carolina Art Association

With James S. Gibbes's bequest, trustees for the Carolina Art Association purchased a lot at 135 Meeting Street and hired a renowned South Carolina architect, Frank P. Milburn, to design a gallery. The building that showcased art would itself need to be a showcase. Milburn chose the Beaux-Arts style that included a Tiffany-style stained-glass dome and classical elements in the exterior.

The building opened to the public on April 11, 1905. It was named the James S. Gibbes Memorial Art Gallery after the man whose legacy enabled the association and the city to continue an appreciation for and education of the arts.

Soon the name changed to the Gibbes Art Gallery. The association and the gallery concentrated on collecting American art with a focus on Charleston and the Lowcountry.

In 1920, the Sketch Club, an auxiliary group of the Gibbes that had formed in 1912, established a studio art school at the Gibbes, with artist Alfred Hutty as its first director.

In 1936, the Gibbes made international history when it hosted the first-ever public showing of Solomon Guggenheim's collection of modern art. The exhibition featured 128 original works from artists such as Rudolf Bauer, Marc Chagall, Fernand Leger, Vasily Kandinsky, and Pablo Picasso.

In 1969, the Gibbes School of Art opened on 76 Queen Street. In 1972, the Gibbes received accreditation from the American Association of Museums. In 1988 the name of the organization changed again to the Gibbes Museum of Art.

Over the years, the Gibbes has housed a collection of more than five hundred paintings, including works by many nationally prominent artists. The museum also maintains a collection of eighteenth- and nineteenth-century miniature portraits and a collection of contemporary art. Other collections include the Marks Collection of early-twentieth-century photographs, the Read Japanese Print Collection, and the Ballard Collection of European prints and drawings.

Gibbes Museum, 1905 *Library of Congress*

RESURGENCE OF THE PERFORMING ARTS

Charleston, once the city with the best music and theater the country had to offer, was silenced during the Civil War and Reconstruction, with the notable exception of the Academy of Music. It wasn't until the Charleston Renaissance that she found her voice again.

Music

At this point in Charleston's history, festivals, musicals, and concerts were offered primarily as entertainment, but they were also a field of study and given on occasion to raise awareness or funds for various causes.

ORCHESTRAS

In 1919, four Charleston women gathered to promote musical arts.

They were led by Maud Winthrop Gibbon. Born into a wealthy family, Gibbon had studied the cello in New York and had traveled abroad. She returned to Charleston in 1917 and began to promote the Musical Arts Club. She was joined by Martha Laurens Patterson, a church organist; Marie Baker, a violin teacher at Ashley Hall School; and Dr. Mary V. McBee, Ashley Hall School's principal.

Their efforts resulted in the Charleston Museum Society, which offered subscription concerts on Sundays featuring amateur and professional talent. Patterson was the first conductor of this group. Having a woman in this role was a significant detail, given that this was the year before women were granted the right to vote.

Within two years, 1921, they had formed the Charleston Symphony Orchestra, and the next year, Gibbon organized a youth orchestra and began promoting music education in Charleston's public schools, assisted by a gentleman with passion for musical arts equal to their own.

Theodore Wichmann graduated from the Chicago Musical College in 1922 and in 1925 founded the Philharmonic Symphony Orchestra of Charleston. The orchestra was performed in the Dock Street Theatre, the Memminger Auditorium, and the Gaillard Auditorium and was conducted by the likes of J. Albert Fracht, Tony Hadgi, and Don Mills.

For decades Wichmann was in the role of instrumental music director of the public schools. Many of his students went on to become members of either his or Gibbon's orchestra. He organized the Brass and Reed Choir, the Charleston High School Band, the Charleston High School Orchestra, and the Public School Orchestra. He also gave private music lessons.

By the end of the 1920s, economic difficulties (primarily the stock market crash) caused the musical activities to falter. Gibbons left Charleston, returning in the mid-1930s. She and Patterson formed the Charleston String Orchestra in 1936. The organization expanded and by 1942 again was called the Charleston Symphony Orchestra.

The Charleston Symphony Orchestra gave its first concert on December 7, 1942. That same year, Wichmann's orchestra dwindled when its volunteer members were called to civilian and military duties.

THE CRADLE OF JAZZ

The Jenkins Orphanage Band was formed in the late 1800s to help support the home, and at first, they played on street corners in town, passing the hat for money.

But then their reputation grew, and along with it, the opportunities came rolling in.

The band had its own stage at the St. Louis World's Fair in 1904. The next year, they were invited to play for President Theodore Roosevelt's inauguration, an honor they repeated in 1909 for President Taft.

In 1914, they received free transportation to London to play at the Anglo-American Exposition—with new uniforms. Over the next few years, the band traveled to Austria, England, France, Germany, and Italy. And years later, the band performed on Broadway for the entire original run of DuBose and Dorothy Heyward's play, *Porgy*.

To increase revenue, Jenkins sent out several bands on tour—five each summer and two each winter—spreading the "Charleston Sound" far and wide, and their exposure increased. In this way, they were a direct contributor, if not the impetus, for the American jazz scene.

Their unique musical style—in particular, the dance craze "The Charleston"—helped usher in the flappers and dappers of the Jazz Age.

By the 1920s, the orphanage had become *the* place for Charleston musicians to meet and jam, and many non-orphans auditioned for the band. The better musicians were allowed to join.

Musician and artist Merton Simpson recalled that "everybody wanted to go there just because it was such a good place to get involved with music. Charleston was at that time a kind of musical center for jazz."

Several alumni of the Jenkins Orphanage Band went on to the big time, including Jabbo Smith, Freddie Green, Tom Delaney, and William "Cat" Anderson. Jazz greats also played with the band when touring South Carolina, among them Duke Ellington, Count Basie, Dizzy Gillespie, and Lionel Hampton. (For more info on the Jenkins Orphanage Band and how it started, see page 146.)

Jenkins was proud not only of the children's performances but also their progress into productive adults. In an interview with *Time* magazine in 1935, he bragged that of the thousands of children who had passed through the orphanage since 1891, fewer than ten had ended up in prison.

After Jenkins's death in 1937, the orphanage relocated from downtown Charleston to North Charleston, on a plot of land on the Ashley River.

The band trips continued into the 1950s, but eventually ended altogether.

Today, the orphanage operates as the Jenkins Institute for Children and continues to provide services and activities for boys and girls in the community.

The Jenkins Orphanage Band *Courtesy of Jenkins Institute*

The Band Does the Charleston

Along with their influence on jazz, it is widely believed that the Jenkins Orphanage Band helped spread the dance craze known as "The Charleston."

A 1924 newspaper in Harlem mentions dance steps by boys—specifically "street urchins"—who appeared on street corners giving dance exhibitions for loose change. With the band's migrations into the northern states for fundraising, it is likely that these "urchins" were with the band.

Surviving documents of the band's early years—including photographs, moving pictures, and personal recollections from band members—all show that footwork was a key element of the band's routine.

The bandleader was the star of the show, usually standing in front of the band, dancing and waving arms in time with the music, putting on a show for the audience.

The fancy footwork was the basis for The Charleston dance phenomenon. The local newspaper followed the New York papers with its own report.

"Something new in the way of advertising for Charleston is developing quite rapidly in New York," said the Charleston Evening Post *in early November 1924, "and, if it follows the usual course, will in due time become the newest rage in the terpsichorean art."*

AMERICAN OPERA

The parents of DuBose Heyward were aristocrats from the upstate, made homeless by the Civil War, who came to Charleston in 1885 to better their lives. Along with many other once-powerful families in Charleston that had been reduced to genteel poverty by the war, Heyward's father made a living in a rice mill. He died in an industrial accident when DuBose was three, at which point his mother became the sole breadwinner.

She took in sewing, ran a boardinghouse on Sullivan's Island, and wrote down Gullah folktales she'd known as a young girl to perform them for local arts groups. The immersion in the Gullah world made an impact on Heyward, but his plans for a career in art were hindered by a series of illnesses, the most devastating of which was polio.

With no college education, he went into the insurance business with a partner. The agency was successful, which gave Heyward more time for his first love: poetry writing. In 1920, along with others he founded the Poetry Society of South Carolina, an organization that helped initiate the southern literary renaissance of the early twentieth century.

Through the organization, he met literary figures such as Carl Sandburg and Amy Lowell and gained access to the New Hampshire artists' retreat, the MacDowell Colony, where he met his future wife, Dorothy Hartzell Kuhns, a playwright. Soon after their wedding, she convinced him to throw over the insurance business for full-time writing. He took her advice and in 1925 wrote *Porgy*, a novel about African-American life set in the 1920s in a fictional Charleston settlement called Catfish Row, based on Cabbage Row, located around the corner from his house on Tradd Street. His protagonist was a crippled beggar.

The book changed literary depictions of Blacks in the United States forever, with a white southerner presenting African Americans in an honest and realistic way rather than the stereotyped portrayals usually found in antebellum narratives.

Though he was ostracized (to a small degree) from Charleston society for the book, he scored points with the New York literary world, who applauded him for his courage in writing it.

Dorothy Heyward saw dramatic possibilities in the story and convinced DuBose that it would work as a play. With his wife's stagecraft, DuBose brought a nonmusical version of *Porgy* to the theater, which created dramatic roles for

Heyward-Washington House and Cabbage Row postcard drawn by Elizabeth O'Neill Verner *Courtesy of South Caroliniana Library, University of South Carolina, SC*

African-American actors and showcased their talents beyond the vaudevillian character of most African-American stage works at the time.

The couple collaborated on the adaptation, making sure that the play's company be cast with only African-American actors. This was controversial at the time, when Black characters were almost always portrayed by white actors in blackface. The play was a huge success, running for 367 performances.

A few years later, the innovative opera *Porgy and Bess* made its debut. DuBose had a role in the composition and production. He collaborated with George Gershwin on the script, wrote the libretto, and authored the lyrics (alone or with Ira Gershwin) to half its songs.

DuBose spent the next several years as resident dramatist of the Dock Street Theatre, newly restored in 1937, where he promoted local playwriting talent. *Porgy and Bess*, the work that brought him and his city fame, was not performed in Charleston until the South Carolina Tricentennial in June 1970, thirty years after his death. He was posthumously inducted into the South Carolina Academy of Authors in 1987.

As for Dorothy's career, she wrote many plays and novels, most of which did not achieve the same level of success as *Porgy*.

Theater

Much like the silencing of music, the "Late Unpleasantness" had darkened local theater for a while. The Charleston Renaissance brought the favorite pastime back to life, and, once a heartbeat was felt, it showed how much it was alive and kicking.

DOCK STREET THEATRE REBORN

The theater-turned-hotel was forced to close during the Civil War but reopened soon after. Reconstruction was not kind to the hotel, and by 1885, it was used as a cheap tenement. By the 1930s, it was uninhabitable and slated for demolition.

Local preservationists urged then-mayor Burnet Maybank to have the city buy the property and restore it through the Works Progress Administration as part of President Roosevelt's New Deal. The plan was for the new theater to be modeled on eighteenth-century London playhouses. Construction began in 1935.

The theater was built within the shell of the former hotel, with the auditorium going up in the courtyard area. The hotel's grand foyer became the grand foyer of the theater, and the dining room became the box-office lobby.

Dock Street Theatre interior, 1936 *Photographs by Frances Benjamin Johnston. Library of Congress*

Local carpenters used locally grown and milled native black cypress for the wooden interiors. Other interior features included decorative plasterwork and Adamesque woodwork that were salvaged from the Radcliffe-King Mansion (circa 1799), which had stood at the intersection of George and Meeting Streets. That structure had been built in 1802 but was demolished in 1935 and replaced with the College of Charleston gymnasium.

Following the $350,000 renovation, the Dock Street Theatre, renamed for the original theater built on Dock Street (renamed Queen Street), held its second grand opening on November 26, 1937.

As a tribute to Charleston's love of history, the first performance was *The Recruiting Officer*, the first play performed in the original theater in 1736. Notables in the audience included author DuBose Heyward, who was named writer-in-residence.

The Dock Street Theatre has remained a popular venue for local theater, offering its stage for performances in various festivals, including the Spoleto Festival USA, an international arts festival that spans seventeen days in May/June.

GLORIA THEATER / SOTTILE THEATRE

In 1927, Albert Sottile opened the Gloria Theater with an entrance on King Street. It was used as a showcase for Sottile's Pastime Amusement Company's vaudeville, touring shows, and movies. The Gloria was designed to mimic the great movie palaces of the time. It was known for its opulent design and architecture, with an illuminated blue dome and twinkling stars in the ceiling.

Originally fitted with two thousand seats, it was the largest theater of its kind in the state. The Gloria was the third of fourteen theaters opened by Sottile's company in and around the King Street area between 1925 and 1931.

In its early years, the theater was primarily a movie house. Its opening night showing on August 19, 1927, was the silent film After Midnight starring Norma Shearer. A decade later, the South Carolina premiere of *Gone with the Wind* was held at the Gloria. Members of the original cast were in attendance, including Charleston native Alicia Rhett, who played India Wilkes in the film.

In later years, as larger, more modern movie theaters opened with a wider variety and multiple screens, the Gloria was unable to compete and closed its doors in 1975. Soon after it was purchased by the College of Charleston and, after years in disuse, it went through extensive renovations—which included restoring the dome, twinkling stars, and decorative plasterwork—and reopened in February 1990 and was renamed the Sottile Theatre, with its entrance moved to George Street.

Artwork Discovered

During later renovations to the Sottile in 2011, two large murals were discovered beneath acoustic tiles. The murals had been painted during original construction in the 1920s. Not much was known about the paintings or the artists. However, a clue was found in an article in the August 20, 1927, edition of the Charleston Evening Post *that mentioned the theater's opening. The article's title was: "Gloria Theater admired by throngs at opening performances Saturday."*

"The wall paintings, classical in concept were done by Italian artists from New York, who executed their work on canvas here. One depicts the Centaur and nymphs, with an attractive landscape background and the other suggests music and drama. On either side of these canvases are fine ornamental panels. And even the exits are pleasing to the eye for they are under large garden cabinets in which the foliage blends most fittingly with the scenery of the paintings. The general color effect of the interiors is featured by gold and buff but with other subdued shades that harmonize."

The art department at the College of Charleston has undertaken the task of restoring the murals. The restoration work includes remediation of the spots of tar that had been used to attach the acoustic tiles to the murals. The south mural had to be removed temporarily because of severe damage, but the north mural was left uncovered, with its damage on display to patrons.

THE RIVIERA THEATRE

Albert Sottile's Pastime Amusement Company acquired the Academy of Music (see Section 4: The Late Unpleasantness) building in 1920, but it wasn't until 1936 that he decided to demolish it and rebuild.

The Academy of Music's replacement was a movie theater with 1,193 seats (789 in orchestra level, 125 in balcony, 279 in rear balcony/gallery) designed in art deco style. It opened in January 1939 and showed first-run movies on its fifty-foot screen.

The theater closed in 1977 and was almost demolished until a group called Friends of the Riviera raised awareness of the need for its rehabilitation. The Charleston Place Hotel (now the Belmont Charleston Place) bought it in the 1990s and turned it into a conference and convention venue. It was declared a National Historic Landmark in 1973 and retains much of its original wall murals and art deco features.

Riviera Theatre present day *Point North Images*

OTHER NOTEWORTHY THEATERS

During this time, entertainment was making a serious comeback. Theater owners and production companies rushed to get in on the action. Most of the following venues took advantage of the new motion picture industry; others continued with vaudeville-type fare.

Theatorium, 1907, 321 King Street. This theater had a brief life: opened in 1907 and closed in 1908.

Wonderland Theatre, 1907, 249 King Street. This theater had several penny-operated stereopticon machines in the front with a one-hundred-seat live theater in the back. In 1908 talking pictures were introduced, and an organ was added. Today the location is retail space.

Cameo Theatre, 1908, 343 King Street. This theater operated until 1950 and was demolished in 1951.

Victory Theater, 1911, 86 Society Street. One of the few theaters not on King Street, it originally had nine hundred seats and was remodeled to hold 1,850 seats. It closed in 1945.

Crescent Theatre, 1913, 617 King Street. The same manager ran the Dixieland Theatre across the street. The Crescent closed in 1919 and has since been demolished.

Dixieland Theatre, 1913, 616 King Street. This theater, operated by the same manager as the Crescent Theatre across the street, catered to an African-American audience, with ads saying, "Pretty Girls, Funny Comedians, and the Latest in Moving Pictures." In 1920 the manager closed it and opened the Milo Theatre a block away. This venue was leased for a while to the Charleston Philharmonic Society. It was remodeled several years later and reopened as the Palace Theatre, but it was eventually demolished in 1968.

Princess Theatre, 1913, 304 King Street. Open until 1927, it has had several uses and today is home to a sports bar.

Garden Theatre, 1918, 371 King Street. Initially opened as a vaudeville house a few doors down from the Riviera, it was converted to a movie theater and ran until the 1970s. It closed for a while and was restored in 1977. During the 1980s, it was used as a venue for Spoleto Festival performances and later repurposed as a performing arts space. The City of Charleston did not renew its lease in 2003, and it was eventually converted into retail space.

Lincoln Theatre, 1920, 601 King Street. This theater catered to African-American audiences and featured live shows and movies. It closed in the 1970s and was demolished following heavy damage from Hurricane Hugo in 1989.

Milo Theatre, 1921, 566 King Street. The manager also owned the Crescent and the Dixieland theaters. This theater catered to African-American audiences. It closed sometime in the 1930s.

Carolina Theatre, 1932, 399 King Street. This venue was decorated in Modernistic style and seated 450. It has since been demolished.

American Theatre, 1942, 446 King Street. Decorated in art moderne style, for a while it offered movies with dining. It has since been converted into a conference hall.

THE POLITICS OF ENTERTAINING AND BEING ENTERTAINED

Charleston was a favorite for many US presidents, before and after the rift-causing secession before the Civil War.

During his southern tour in 1791, President Washington was wined and dined by the city as only Charlestonians can do it (see Section 2: Becoming America), and by all accounts he was both enchanted and exhausted before it was over.

President James Monroe visited Charleston in 1819, attending the theater (at the Broad Street/Charleston Theatre) and staying at St. Andrew's Hall.

The Charleston Hotel's opulence drew in three US presidents—Theodore Roosevelt, William Taft, and Calvin Coolidge. The luxurious Villa Margherita hosted Grover Cleveland, Theodore Roosevelt, and William Taft.

President Franklin Delano Roosevelt spent a significant amount of time in the Charleston area. He was often a guest of Charleston mayor Burnet Maybank. On one of his visits, he visited The Citadel, and when he took a cruise to South America, his ship departed from Charleston. Several times during World War II, Roosevelt visited his friend Bernard Baruch and his daughter, Belle Baruch, at their home in Hobcaw Barony (north of Charleston). Toward the end of the war, he vacationed there for four weeks, the longest vacation in all of his terms.

And years before he was president, John F. Kennedy was stationed in Charleston during his time in the US Navy. At that time, he found entertainment at one of the city's hotels with a Danish immigrant who at the time was suspected to be a Nazi spy. Their room at the Fort Sumter Hotel was bugged by the FBI, and an agent followed them around town. (Obviously, the affair did not last. The romance was broken off, and Kennedy headed off to command a PT boat.)

Politics at Hobcaw

Other political figures were drawn to the area as well. In 1905, Bernard Baruch purchased Hobcaw Barony, a plantation in the Georgetown area, north of Charleston. Baruch was heavily involved in politics: advisor to seven US presidents and other foreign dignitaries, a lifelong friend to Winston Churchill, and a close friend of

Top: Bernard Baruch and his
daughter Belle Baruch at the
Belmont Park Terminal Track
in Belmont, New York, circa
1915 *Library of Congress*

Left: Bernard Baruch at the
White House, 1936
Library of Congress

President Franklin D. Roosevelt before and during his presidency. Churchill frequently visited Hobcaw on vacation and spent considerable time there in 1932 after recuperating in the Bahamas from being struck by a car in New York City.

Some of the entertainment remained more erudite, especially at Hobcaw Barony, where politics was at the forefront. Back in 1935, Bernard Baruch sold five thousand acres of Hobcaw to his oldest daughter, Belle Baruch, who was well known in social circles throughout the country and in Europe. She hosted much of the socialite entertaining during this time, which included the occasional visit from the commander-in-chief.

Postwar Celebrations at Medway

Another Charleston socialite made headlines during the World War II years. Gertrude Sanford Legendre, owner of Medway Plantation outside of Charleston, served in the OSS (Office of Strategic Services) during the war, often entertaining the top brass at her townhome in Washington.

Legendre was transferred to Paris and later was the first American woman in uniform captured in Germany. She was a prisoner of war for six months and eventually escaped on a train to Switzerland. After the war, she used her home at Medway Plantation to help with the postwar effort. Thereafter, every year until her death, she held a party on New Year's Eve attended by socialites and businesspeople in Charleston and dignitaries from other areas of the country.

Invention of She-Crab Soup

Creative cuisine continued long after Reconstruction. One fine example involved a visit from the president of the United States. There are several versions of this story, one of which goes like this:

President Taft was good friends with Charleston's then-mayor R. Goodwyn Rhett and visited Charleston often between 1908 and 1912, staying at Rhett's home (now the John Rutledge House Inn). During one of the visits, Rhett's cook had planned to serve turtle soup, one of Taft's favorites, but he didn't have all the ingredients on hand, so he opted for crab soup instead. Given that he was cooking for the president, he decided to soup-up the standard crab soup by adding crab roe (or crab eggs) to the dish—and she-crab soup was born. The she-crabs (roe-carrying female crabs) are a delicacy, having a better taste than the male crab counterparts, and the orange eggs give the dish more flavor and color. Reportedly, Taft loved the soup and brought the recipe back to the White House.

John Rutledge House Inn's She-Crab Soup Recipe

5 tablespoons butter
½ cup finely chopped celery
2 cups crab meat
3½ cups milk
½ cup chicken stock
5 tablespoons flour
⅔ teaspoon mace
¼ teaspoon white pepper
1 cup heavy cream
¼ cup Worcestershire
3 tablespoons dry sherry
Salt if necessary, to taste
Optional: 2 hard-boiled egg yolks, grated + paprika

Heat butter in a large saucepan. Add celery, mace and white pepper. Cook over low heat until celery is almost transparent. While celery is cooking, heat milk and chicken stock in a small pan just enough to make milk hot without boiling. When celery mix is done, add flour to make a roux. Do not brown but heat enough to bubble for several minutes. Slowly add milk and chicken stock to the roux, add salt for taste. Add crab meat, heavy cream, Worcestershire, and sherry. Simmer for 30 minutes or until thickened to the appropriate consistency. For a garnish boil 2 eggs. Take the yolk out and grate. Sprinkle over the tops with paprika.

* Note: Because she-crabs are difficult to find in some parts of the country, this recipe is altered slightly from the original. Used with permission.

PRESERVING AND EXPANDING

Even from her earlier years, Charleston struggled to maintain a balancing act between holding the status quo and expanding to reach full potential.

This was never more true than in the years of the Charleston Renaissance. With artists flocking to the area, Charleston was certainly becoming a popular destination. The conundrum was how to keep the area the historic locale that visitors sought out while being modern enough to invite them in.

Holding to Tradition

In 1920, Charleston activist Susan Pringle Frost began soliciting public support to save the 1802 Joseph Manigault House, which was slated for demolition at the time. A few months later, thirty-two concerned citizens met and agreed to fight for the preservation of Charleston. The Society for the Preservation of Old Dwellings was born. It was later chartered as a membership organization "to preserve old dwellings having historical association from destruction."

With a growing concern for maintaining her historical charm, the society persuaded City Council to adopt what would become the nation's first zoning ordinance to protect historical resources. The ordinance also designated a 138-acre "Old and Historic District" and established a Board of Architectural Review.

In the same year, the society was renamed the Preservation Society of Charleston in recognition of its role in protecting dwellings, buildings, sites, and cultural landmarks. It was the first organization of its kind in America.

The society wisely combined preservation with entertainment, hosting tours, symposiums, and events, continuing to do so today.

Later, the society instituted the Carolopolis Award program—awarding plaques to place on specific buildings—to recognize preservation excellence in Charleston and began its Historic Markers program.

Becoming a Tourist Magnet

Charleston as a tourist destination became more of a reality with the opening of the Cooper River Bridge in 1929, which helped traffic along King's Highway (later US 17).

At this point, Charleston Hotel still struggled to maintain her dignity despite the effects of Reconstruction and the Distillery Act. Other hotels were built to accommodate the influx of visitors, and they provided bars and dining rooms that were enjoyed by residents year-round. Some of the more famous of these hotels include the following.

THE ARGYLE HOTEL

The Argyle was converted from the St. Charles Hotel in 1901, just in time for the South Carolina Inter-State and West Indian Exposition.

Being across from the infamous and elegant Charleston Hotel was a challenge for the Argyle, which was met by having meals included with the price of a room.

A few years later, the hotel hired a manager who aimed for the hotel to become the city's "first and only modern European-plan hotel," selling menu items a la carte to attract theater patrons and train passengers.

Argyle Hotel postcard *Courtesy of South Caroliniana Library, University of South Carolina, SC*

Like many other hotels, the Argyle ran into difficulties during the Great Depression, and in 1957, the building was razed.

ST. JOHN HOTEL

During the Civil War, Otis Mills sold the bulk of his real estate and invested in Confederate bonds. That included the Mills House, which he sold for $13,500 Confederate dollars.

For the next few decades, the hotel's operation is unclear, though it's certain that in 1871 the hotel was sold at auction, with several subsequent transactions, and eventually made its way to Cecilia Lawton, owner of Battery Dairy, a milk bottler and distributor downtown. She renamed the Mills House "St. John Hotel" after her son. She sold the property in 1907, though the buyers kept the name for decades.

At this point, the hotel was used to accommodating large banquets and was regularly rented out to groups such as the South Carolina Kindergarten Association and St. Andrew's Society.

Even with Charleston's growing tourism and the resurgence in banquets, St. John Hotel suffered from competition from the new Francis Marion and Fort Sumter hotels. The dilapidated structure was sold at public auction in 1968. The new owners decided to demolish it and replace it with a close replica, increasing from five stories to seven. The original iron balcony was salvaged. The original terra-cotta window pediments were stored in the basement of Hibernian Hall so reproductions could be cast. The new Mills House Hotel registered its first guests on October 9, 1970.

THE COMMERCIAL CLUB / TIMROD HOTEL

The Commercial Club, located on Meeting Street between the County Courthouse and Hibernian Hall, grew out of the entrepreneurial drive that occurred during the South Carolina Inter-State and West Indian Expo. The building had been a row of four attached tenements built in the late nineteenth century and remodeled in 1904 as a residential/businessmen's clubhouse.

The Commercial Club was designed to promote business and industrial growth in Charleston. Its organizers thought that by housing business professionals together, the resulting conversations and activities would stimulate collaboration.

The club's earliest members were the Charleston Chamber of Commerce (the nation's first), the Cotton Exchange, the Merchants Exchange, the Young Businessmen's League, and a new Real Estate Exchange.

Commercial Club postcard *Wikimedia Commons*

The first floor of the club had a barbershop, coffee shop, drugstore, and haberdashery. The second floor contained one large and two smaller dining rooms, a restaurant, rooms for reading, a billiards room, a bowling room, and rooms for ping pong and shuffleboard. The third floor held a roof garden and banquet hall, and the fourth floor was enclosed in glass, which the *Evening Post* noted in one of its articles, could be opened "making a delightful resort to spend the evenings during the summer months."

In 1918 the clubhouse converted into the Timrod Inn (and known later as Timrod Hotel). Over the next four decades, the essence of the Commercial Club continued, as many of the city's politicians and lawyers met in the hotel's coffee shop every morning. It's said that many of the biggest deals in the city were made there.

The property changed hands several times over the years and closed in 1955. The building was demolished in 1964 to make way for the County Office Building.

FRANCIS MARION HOTEL

The Francis Marion Hotel opened in 1924 at King and Calhoun Streets, facing Marion Square, in the heart of the retail shopping district.

In the 1920s, the Charleston Renaissance was in full swing, and in the gilded moment, the Francis Marion Hotel was the place to be.

Frances Marion Hotel postcard *Courtesy of South Caroliniana Library, University of South Carolina, SC*

The hotel, named for the Revolutionary War hero Francis Marion, the "Swamp Fox," boasted from its grand opening that it provided "gracious service, elegant accommodations, and splendid banquets and events." The Swamp Fox Restaurant, a favorite of residents, has been offering classic southern cuisine since the hotel's launch.

At twelve stories, one of the highest buildings on the peninsula, many of the hotel's 235 guestrooms and suites offer stunning views of the harbor and a close view of the city's church-steeple skyline.

The hotel was renovated in 1996 with a $12 million National Trust for Historic Preservation award-winning restoration. The upgrade combined 1920s style with twenty-first-century comfort and convenience.

FORT SUMTER HOTEL

Situated at 1 King Street, in an exclusive residential area adjacent to the Battery and White Point Garden, Fort Sumter Hotel opened to guests in 1924. At that time, the seven-story structure was the tallest luxury hotel on the Charleston Peninsula and was designed in a Spanish Colonial style.

A 1929 brochure bragged that its "spacious lobbies, sun parlors and terraces, comfortable and luxuriously furnished, overlook the water and offer cordial hospitality in an atmosphere to be found in few hotels." At that time, a dock beside the hotel stretched into the harbor, allowing berthing for yachts.

The ground floor featured a dining room that for many years was one of the downtown area's few restaurants. By the 1950s, it hyped its air conditioning and "manufactured ice" in drinks. The second floor included a grand ballroom and lounge.

Between 1942 and 1946, the hotel served as headquarters for the Sixth Naval District prior to its move to the Navy Base. At that point, the building was remodeled and returned to hotel operation.

In 1947, playwright Tennessee Williams and agent Audrey Wood met with Producer Irene Selznick at the hotel to discuss the production of his newest play, *A Streetcar Named Desire*. Williams had hand-written some of the scenes on the hotel's stationery.

Through the 1950s, artist Alfred Hutty's paintings and etchings were on permanent exhibit in the hotel. His 1949 mural "Attack on Fort Sumter" still hangs in the hotel lobby today.

The hotel closed in 1973 and was converted into condominiums.

VILLA MARGHERITA

This hotel was originally built as a private residence but functioned as a small hotel from 1905 until 1953. Guests included Sinclair Lewis, who worked on his novel *Main Street* here (and mentions it in his text); Alexander Graham Bell; Henry Ford; and several writers, including Gertrude Stein, who was passing through Charleston. While here, Stein delivered a lecture for the Poetry Society of Charleston at the South Carolina Society Hall. Villa Margherita also hosted three American presidents: Grover Cleveland, Theodore Roosevelt, and William Taft.

Villa Margherita then and now *Library of Congress*

Point North Images

WIDE OPEN SPACES

During this time, the great outdoors continued to offer diversions for both locals and tourists, and the diversions were plentiful.

Gardens

The gardens in Charleston and surrounding areas were thoughtfully, and in some places professionally, designed. Loutrel Briggs, a landscape architect from New York, began a landscape practice to cater to wealthy New Yorkers who "wintered" in Charleston. His first commission was for Mrs. Washington Roebling, widow of the engineer of the Brooklyn Bridge, at her home on South Battery (beside White Point Garden).

Another of Briggs's famous gardens is at 58 Church Street, the subject of the New York Times bestseller, *Mrs. Whaley and Her Charleston Garden.*

While the massive gardens on the plantations were famous (more so by the day), the tiny pieces of land beside and behind the homes in the city were elegant and enchanting. Briggs designed more than one hundred of these gardens in Charleston.

Library of Congress

He also landscaped a property in nearby Moncks Corner called Mepkin Garden, owned by Henry and Clare Boothe Luce. The Luces later donated a large part of the property, including the gardens Briggs designed, to an order of Trappist monks, at which point it became Mepkin Abbey.

GARDEN CLUB AND GATEWAY WALK

Founded in 1922 and federated in 1932, the Garden Club of Charleston is one of the oldest and largest garden clubs in America. Members offer tours of private homes and gardens in the downtown area and have funded many community projects through the years.

Among its beautification projects is the grounds of the Charleston Library Society at 164 King Street.

Another special project was the Gateway Walk, which came about after the Garden Club president's trip to Paris, where he visited peaceful gardens throughout the city. When he returned to Charleston, he contracted with Loutrell Briggs to design a city nature walk in the heart of Charleston. The walk was completed in 1930 to coincide with the commemoration of Charles Town's 250th anniversary.

The walk begins at the gates of St. John's Lutheran Church on Archdale Street, crosses King Street and Meeting Street, and concludes at St. Philip's on Church

Gateway Walk *Point North Image*

Street. The walk is marked with the brass medallions sealed into the sidewalks at various points.

BROOKGREEN GARDENS

The acreage that comprises Brookgreen Gardens, north of Charleston, was once home to four separate rice plantations: The Oaks, Brookgreen, Springfield, and Laurel Hill.

When Archer and Anna Hyatt Huntington purchased the 9,100 acres in 1930, it was meant to be a retreat for Anna, a noted sculptor, while she recovered from tuberculosis. However, Anna saw the potential for the property—stretching from the Atlantic Ocean to the Waccamaw River—to be a showcase for her sculptures, and within a year, the Huntingtons incorporated the property as a private, not-for-profit entity. Anna's vision was soon expanded to include other sculptures.

The Huntingtons oversaw the development of the site and opened it to the public the following year. From the beginning, Brookgreen was intended to be a showcase of art and nature, where monumental works of art could be displayed against the majestic live oaks.

Today, Brookgreen is best known for its display gardens and American figurative sculpture collection. More than 550 pieces of sculpture are displayed in an outdoor setting, situated with plants and native flowers that have been selected to set off the classic lines of marble, bronze, and gold-leaf sculptures, highlighted by ponds and fountains.

Part of the property has been designated a wildlife preserve, with native animals roaming the trails. The site is accredited by the American Association of Museums and was designated a National Historic Landmark in 1992.

HAMPTON PARK

After the purchase of the Washington Race Course, the city turned the area into Hampton Park, retaining the sunken gardens, gazebo, and other elements of the 1901–1902 expo.

It became a hugely popular site thanks in part to a donation from Archer Huntington, owner of Brookgreen Gardens, who visited in 1937. He gave some exotic birds and monkeys that had been hanging around Brookgreen. That started the formal zoo, which included bison, otters, bears, lions, and other animals. The zoo included two aviaries, one of which was converted from the park's old trolley station.

Hampton Park postcards *Courtesy of South Caroliniana Library, University of South Carolina, SC*

In the 1970s, the zoo was unable to renovate and expand its facilities and was forced to close. Most of the animals were sent to the then-new Charles Towne Landing site, and the remaining were sent to zoos around the country. Hampton Park was removed into the greenspace park that it is today.

Sport Revivals

Gardens weren't the only activity beckoning everyone outdoors. Some of the previously venerated sports bounced back, though in different forms than before, and other open-air activities launched.

After the Civil War and Reconstruction, the locals may have had little money, but they had plenty of land and, for some, historic homes to go with it. This allowed the residents to partner with wealthy visitors from the north to create venues for their favorite sports.

REMNANTS OF THE JOCKEY CLUB

Though the Jockey Club was no more, the love of the sport still burned hot. The Charleston tracks moved farther away, into the center of the state.

Aiken, west of Charleston, became a popular location for steeplechasing in 1930, followed by harness racing in 1936, and flat racing in 1942. These events continue today as Aiken's Triple Crown in the spring. Aiken also hosts a fall steeplechase meet.

In Camden, a new Springdale Race Course in 1930 birthed the Carolina Cup Race Meet for steeplechasers. Wrenfield, a flat track built in 1936, hosted a few days of trials. Later the Colonial Cup was added to the venue at Springdale. Both events continue today as significant stops on the steeplechase circuit.

In the 1940s, an active South Carolina Turf Club held a circuit in the South Carolina midlands towns of Newberry, Eutawville, Summerville, St. Matthews, St. Johns, Colleton, Williamsburg, Elloree, and Camden.

The charter of the South Carolina Jockey Club charter was revived in 1984, and in 1986, horse racing finally returned to Charleston with the creation of the Charleston Cup steeplechase races at Stono Ferry Plantation, just south of Charleston.

GOLF REBOUNDS

In 1895, the City of Charleston purchased two plantations—six hundred acres— along the Cooper River to create Chicora Park as a day destination for wealthy Charlestonians.

On October 1, 1900, the Chicora Golf Club officially formed at Chicora Park. The first course was a nine-hole golf course at Chicora Park. In May 1901, the city sold the land to the US Navy for the development of the Charleston Naval Base and used the money to acquire Washington Race Course and develop Hampton Park.

Chicora Park, 1890 *Library of Congress*

The Chicora Golf Club moved on, purchasing the Belvidere Plantation, located on the west bank of the Cooper River (just north of Magnolia Cemetery in the Charleston Neck area), for its next course. The club laid out a nine-hole course, refurbished the circa 1800 plantation as its clubhouse, and changed its name to the Charleston Country Club.

By 1913, the Belvidere Course had become so popular that the club enlarged to eighteen holes. Membership increased so much that by late 1916, the *News and Courier* reported that applications were "being handed in almost every day. . . . Members having automobiles enjoy making the club a sort of terminal or rendezvous."

For members and guests, the club included not only golfing links, but also tennis courts, golf tournaments for men, bridge parties for women, and teas and dances on Saturday afternoons.

Unfortunately for the club, the property was in an industrial area that was developing fast. The Southern Railway built a coal pier near Belvidere, and Standard Oil Company built tank farms at the north and west.

The club moved again in 1922, this time purchasing 225 acres of high land from the McLeod Plantation on James Island. With the change brought a new name: The Country Club of Charleston. The clubhouse, situated on top of the Civil War era Battery Means, opened in 1925.

Standard Oil Company eventually bought Belvidere and built an oil refinery on the grounds of the old country club. By 1938, the plantation house was in disrepair and was demolished in 1964, though parts of it were salvaged and repurposed in buildings downtown.

Chicora Park evolved into the Navy officers' housing and, after the base closure in 1996, became North Charleston's Riverfront Park, opened to the public in 2005. Today the park includes an outdoor performance venue, picnic areas, a fishing pier, a boardwalk, and a Naval Base Memorial site.

Meanwhile in Hanahan, just north of Charleston, the vision for Yeaman's Hall Club began in 1916 when a nine-hundred-acre piece of land was acquired with plans to develop a winter resort club catering to wealthy northerners traveling south by train to warmer climates.

Belvidere Park *Library of Congress*

Besides two courses, plans included a variety of other leisure activities and amenities as well as 250 homesites available for members to purchase.

For unknown reasons, the project was put on hiatus for several years, but got back on course in 1924 when the club, named after original landowner Sir John Yeamans, officially formed and construction began on the first course. The course opened in 1925.

In the next four years, the club experienced a surge in membership and sales of homesites. When the stock market crashed in 1929, development came to a stop and, in the end, the full scope of the project never materialized.

Today, Yeamans Hall Club is an ultra-private club with one course, a pro shop, a clubhouse, guest cottages, two tennis courts, and only thirty-five homes on the property. The club stays open year-round. During the summer months when few members are using the course, Yeamans Hall Club hosts an association of summer golfers who are able to enjoy the course.

SAILING

With the growing popularity of the Rockville Regatta (see Section 4: The Late Unpleasantness), sailing caught the attention of young and old, rich and poor—and a new club was inevitable.

The Charleston Yacht Club was founded in 1934 when nine men gathered at Adger's Wharf, located at the foot of Tradd Street, with plans to generate an interest in water sports.

In 1936, the club received a grant of land from the Halsey family. (Today this land is near a tidal pool across the boulevard from the present Lockwood Marina.) The original building was a run-down mule barn, but the members made it suitable for a yacht club.

Over the years, the Yacht Club has sponsored a Junior Sailing Program and has instructed hundreds of young sailors, many of whom became leaders in the sailing community. The Junior Sailing Program begat the Charleston Junior Yacht Club, whose membership today consists of local youths from all forms of boating.

The club has sponsored US Sailing Association quarter and semifinal championship regattas and the South Atlantic Yacht Racing Associations Inshore and Offshore Championships. It has also hosted several national championships such as the Mallory National Championship, the Sunfish North Americans, and the Y-Flyer Nationals.

Today the club is a member of the South Atlantic Yacht Racing Association and the US Sailing Association. In 1961, the City Marina moved to the Navy's mine-sweeper fueling facility, and the Charleston Yacht Club was housed in a building on the main dock of the Marina. Membership quickly outgrew that building, and in 1985, the club moved to its present facilities at the City of Charleston Lockwood Municipal Marina.

Surf's Up

As tourism grew, the beaches became even more of an attraction, and the various amusements associated with them expanded. With the exception of Sullivan's Island, the hotel industry flourished on the beaches, even with the economic uncertainties of the times.

ISLE OF PALMS

By 1906, the island had a fifty-room resort hotel that offered overnight accommodations. The Hotel Seashore also served dinner from 1:00 p.m. to 4:00 p.m., with a trolley car available to return visitors to the mainland.

Dr. Lawrence also promoted and later served as president of a company that built more than seven miles of track and trestle for horse-drawn then electric trolley cars to carry visitors from a boat landing in Mount Pleasant all the way to his island paradise.

By 1912, James Sottile's amusement park drew more visitors to the island. The beach pavilion featured a four-hundred-foot dance hall, private dining rooms on the second floor with windows open on three sides to let in the sea breeze, and an open-air observation deck on the rooftop.

By then, a second hotel, Hotel Marion by the Sea, was constructed on the island by the Casey family.

In 1926, the trolley trestle over Breach Inlet was converted into a bridge, which allowed cars to cross from Sullivan's Island to Isle of Palms. Access to Isle of Palms became even easier when the Grace Memorial Bridge replaced the Charleston Harbor ferry in 1929.

With the advent of cars on the island, "horseless carriage" races on the miles of smooth beach sands became a common sport.

In the late 1940s, J. C. Long bought thirteen hundred acres and started developing homes and making improvements, including road construction. Within five years, the resort town of 100 homes had grown to 375 homes, 250 of them occupied year-round.

In 1951, an airstrip and landing field were completed. The pavilion and amusement park later burned and were not replaced. The organized races were outlawed in 1953.

By the 1970s, word about this seaside gem had spread throughout the country and real estate was booming. A beach and racquet club was developed, and in 1985, the landing strip was converted into a golf course. In 1989, Hurricane Hugo destroyed or damaged more than 95 percent of the buildings on the island, causing an estimated $100 million in damages. The island recovered and today has been rebuilt.

SULLIVAN'S ISLAND

The Atlantic Beach Hotel burned on January 9, 1925, along with one of the cottages. The two remaining cottages are still on the island today, though prior to the fire, they had been moved closer to the beach. According to local legend, the fire started when a bootlegger was trying to locate his whiskey in the bushes alongside the hotel and lit a match. His match found the whiskey and sparked the flames.

Though the island continues today to be a resort area, with cottages and homes for summer rental, the Atlantic Beach Hotel was the last one constructed on the island.

FOLLY BEACH

Folly Beach itself provided plenty of amusement. Originally deeded in 1696 as a royal grant, it was isolated from the mainland and became a favorite of pirates. During the Civil War, it was a stronghold for Union forces because of its proximity to Fort Sumter. By the 1920s, it had become a vacation spot, with a pavilion, boardwalk, pier, and oceanfront hotel (and, according to rumors, also a drop-off spot for bootleggers during Prohibition). Gershwin wrote the classic line, "Summertime, and the living is easy" while he stayed on Folly Beach.

Folly Beach is a narrow barrier island south of Charleston, accessible from James Island. It remained undeveloped, with one plantation on the island, until the late nineteenth century. During the Civil War it was used as a staging area for the siege of Battery Wagner (dramatized in the movie *Glory*).

By the early 1900s, northern investors, impressed by the success of the Isle of Palms development, began searching the barrier islands of South Carolina and Georgia for resort locations.

Folly Beach postcards *Courtesy of South Caroliniana Library, University of South Carolina, SC*

In 1919, Folly Island Company purchased the island and planned to develop it into a vacation destination. The company received permission from the state to build a bridge across the Folly River to James Island, and the first cottages were built.

The March 5, 1920, edition of the *News & Courier* called it "one of the most extensive and promising development undertakings launched in this section. . . . The island that was formerly nothing but waste territory is now undergoing a transformation, as well as the water passages and roadways between this beach and Charleston."

The Folly Pier and a boardwalk opened in 1931. The Oceanfront Hotel opened in 1934, the first large facility for overnight guests. For several decades, these were the center of social activity on the island. Restaurants and stores quickly followed.

Arguably the most noted vacationers at Folly during its early years were composer George Gershwin along with DuBose and Dorothy Heyward, who rented a cottage across the street. They spent much of the summer of 1934 on the island collaborating on the opera, *Porgy and Bess.*

The three visited the James Island Gullah communities, where Gershwin was introduced to the native language and music, which gave the foundation for the opera.

By the 1940s, the front beach was a popular destination and came to be known as "The Edge of America." Cars lined the beach in front of the Atlantic Pavilion, where guests could dance to live orchestras, get refreshments at the soda fountain, and visit the bathing house.

In 1957, the pier burned but was replaced, along with the Oceanfront Plaza, which featured a bowling alley, skating rink, and small amusement park that included a rollercoaster, Ferris wheel, and merry-go-round. That pier burned in 1977, and Folly was without one for eighteen years. The current pier was built in 1995 and extends 1,045 feet into the ocean.

SEE FOR YOURSELF: CHARLESTON RENAISSANCE PERIOD

When you're in town, be sure to see where history was made during the Charleston Renaissance period with these tours.

The Gateway Walk

The Gateway Walk gets its name from the wrought iron gates visitors walk through on the route. The walk is an informal trail through some of the gardens and graveyards of Charleston.

The walk is roughly three blocks long, beginning at the gates of St. John's Lutheran Church on Archdale Street, crossing King and Meeting Streets, and concluding at St. Philip's on Church Street.

The walk is free and the path is open, though sometimes the gates are locked or the pathways blocked for various reasons (e.g., outside business hours or during construction). If you find that's the case, you can retrace steps and find an alternate route down an alley that will take you to the next point on the path.

At each point on the path, look for the Gateway Walk bronze plaque embedded in the sidewalk.

Start on Archdale Street at St. John's Lutheran Church. Go through the gates, through the graveyard and into the Unitarian Church's graveyard next door.

Take some time in both graveyards. They have interesting gravestones and monuments in their garden-like state.

Make your way to a gate that leads to a narrow fern-lined walkway. (If St. John's gate is locked, try the Unitarian gate. If it's locked, go a few feet heading toward Queen Street to Jacob's Alley. Along Jacob's Alley, a wall on the left side has a gate that opens onto the same narrow fern-lined walkway.) At the end of the walkway, exit onto King Street.

Be sure to look for the bronze plaque in the sidewalk. The Charleston Library Society will be across the street, slightly to the left.

Cross King Street. The walk continues on the right side of the Society's building.

Behind the Society's building is a shady garden and another gate, which has a plaque on it along with a bronze plaque in the sidewalk.

Go through the gate into the rear of the Gibbes Museum of Art.

This is a formal garden, symmetrical in its design, with tables around the edges and a fountain.

Go to the wrought iron gate at the front left corner of the garden. Cross Meeting Street to the Circular Congregational Church.

You'll know you're on the right track by the bronze plaque in the sidewalk. Go into the churchyard and walk down the brick paths of the ancient cemetery. Like St. John's Lutheran and the Unitarian churchyards, this one has interesting details, gravestones, and monuments. At the back of the churchyard is another gate that leads to St. Philip's Church graveyard.

Go through the gate if it is open. If not (it is often locked), go back to the beginning of the graveyard—but still behind the Circular Congregational Church—and find a side exit from the graveyard and turn right onto Cumberland Street.

Walk toward the big pink steeple, which is St Philip's Episcopal Church. On the way, you'll pass by the Powder Magazine museum on the right. The next street will be Church Street.

Gateway Walk *Point North Images*

Turn right onto Church Street and end the walk at St. Philip's Church. Find the bronze plaque in the sidewalk.

At this point, you are one block away from the City Market, two blocks from East Bay Street (near the US Custom House), and a block from Queen Street.

Walking Tour of the Charleston Renaissance

During the Charleston Renaissance, many of the artists, regardless of medium, often worked together—and it's no wonder, given that they all lived in proximity to one another. This tour highlights a few of them.

Start at the Gibbes Museum of Art.

GIBBES MUSEUM OF ART

135 Meeting St.

The museum opened at this location in 1905. The collection on display on the opening day included more than three hundred pictures, many bronzes, and about two hundred miniatures, along with a variety of Japanese prints.

The museum underwent an extensive two-year, $13.5 million renovation in 2014 and reopened to the public in 2016. The development teams used the original blueprints, discovered in the City of Charleston archives in 2008, to return the building to its 1905 Beaux-Arts–style layout.

Gibbes Museum exterior *Point North Images*

The first floor has classrooms, artist studios, lecture and event spaces, a cafe, and a museum store. The rear reception area opens to the garden, part of Charleston's historic Gateway Walk founded by the Garden Club of Charleston.

The entire ground floor of the museum is admission-free. (For more information on the Gibbes Museum, see page 137 and page 175.)

From the Gibbes building, turn right onto Meeting. Cross Queen and Broad Streets. Turn right and travel two blocks to Legare Street (almost across from the Cathedral of St. John the Baptist). Turn left on Legare Street. Go a block to the corner of Legare and Tradd Streets.

SWORD GATE HOUSE

32 Legare St.

The wall and sword gates might look familiar. This National Historic Landmark was a favorite of artists during the Charleston Renaissance.

Continue down Legare Steet to the Simmons-Edwards House.

SIMMONS-EDWARDS HOUSE

14 Legare St.

At this National Historic Landmark, the pineapple gates—an iconic symbol of Charleston's hospitality—were another favorite of Renaissance artists.

Continue to Lamboll Street and turn left. Go a block to King Street and turn left. Josephine Pinckney's home is on the left.

JOSEPHINE PINCKNEY HOUSE

21 King St.

A few doors down is another National Historic Landmark. It is not associated with the Charleston Renaissance, but it's worth a look as you walk by.

MILES BREWTON HOUSE

27 King St.

An example of a Charleston "double house," this structure was completed in 1769. The house has the distinction of being the headquarters for occupying forces during the Revolutionary War and the Civil War.

Continue up King Street about two blocks to Tradd Street and turn right and cross Meeting Street to the next block of Tradd Street, where more of the Renaissance artists lived.

ALFRED HUTTY HOUSE
46 Tradd St.

ELIZABETH O'NEILL VERNER
HOUSE AND STUDIO
38 Tradd St.
This house was built in 1718 by a barrel-maker and was later used as a "sweet shoppe." Verner used it as her home and art studio.

Verner's house and studio are on the corner of Church Street. Turn right on Church Street, and the DuBose Heyward House will be on the left.

DUBOSE HEYWARD HOUSE
76 Church St.
The house where DuBose and Dorothy Heyward lived from 1919 to 1924 is a National Historic Landmark. It is now a wing of a larger house.

Go back up Church Street, crossing Tradd Street.

ANNA HEYWARD TAYLOR
79 Church St.
A few doors down from Taylor is the Heyward-Washington House. Next to that is a courtyard called Cabbage Row, which was likely the inspiration for the Catfish Row of Heyward's book, *Porgy*.

Cabbage Row *Library of Congress*

A staged production of *Porgy and Bess*, 1935–1936 *Library of Congress*

BIBLIOGRAPHY

Books

Barefoot, Daniel. *Touring South Carolina's Revolutionary War Sites*. Winston-Salem, NC: John F. Blair Publisher, 1999.

Butler, Nicholas Michael. *Votaries of Apollo: The St. Cecilia Society and the Patronage of Concert Music in Charleston, South Carolina, 1766–1820*. Columbia: University of South Carolina Press, 2007.

Chibbaro, Anthony. *The Charleston Exposition*. Charleston: Arcadia Publishing, 2001.

Current, Richard N., T. Harry Williams, and Frank Freidel. *American History: A Survey*. Second Edition. New York: Alfred A. Knopf, 1966.

Davis, Burke. *The Civil War: Strange & Fascinating Facts*. New York: Random House, 1996.

Downey, Christopher Byrd. *Stede Bonnet: Charleston's Gentleman Pirate*. Charleston, SC: The History Press, 2012.

Eastman, Margaret Middleton Rivers. *Hidden History of Old Charleston*. With Edward Fitzsimmons Good. Charleston, SC: The History Press, 2010.

Eberle, Kevin R. *A History of Charleston's Hampton Park*. Charleston, SC: History Press, 2012.

Grun, Bernard. *The Timetables of History*. The New Third Revised Edition. Based upon Werner Stein's *Kulturfahrplan*. New York: Simon & Schuster, 1991.

Hutchisson, James M., and Harland Greene, eds. *Renaissance in Charleston: Art and Life in the Carolina Low Country, 1900–1940*. Athens: University of Georgia Press, 2003.

Irving, John Beaufain. *The South Carolina Jockey Club*. Charleston: Russell & Jones, 1857.

Jones, Mark R. *Charleston Firsts*. Charleston, SC: East Atlantic Publishing, LLC, 2016.

———. *Doin' the Charleston: Black Roots of American Popular Music & the Jenkins Orphanage Legacy*. Charleston, SC: East Atlantic Publishing, LLC, 2013.

————. *Wicked Charleston: The Dark Side of the Holy City*. Charleston, SC: The History Press, 2005.

————. *Wicked Charleston: Volume 2, Prostitutes, Politics and Prohibition*. Charleston, SC: The History Press, 2006.

Marion, John Francis. *The Charleston Story: Scenes from a City's History*. Harrisburg, PA: Stackpole Books, 1978.

McInnis, Maurie D. *The Politics of Taste in Antebellum Charleston*. Chapel Hill: University of North Carolina Press, 2005.

McNeil, Jim. *Charleston's Navy Yard: A Picture History*. Charleston, SC: Coker Craft Press, Inc., 1985.

Reich, Jerome R. *Colonial America*. Third Edition. Englewood Cliffs, NJ: Prentice Hall, Inc. / Simon & Schuster, 1994.

Risjord, Norman K. *Representative Americans: The Colonists*. Lexington, MA: D. C. Heath and Company, 1981.

Rosen, Robert. *A Short History of Charleston*. Columbia: University of South Carolina Press, 1992.

Smith, Alice R. Huger, and D. E. Huger Smith. *The Dwelling Houses of Charleston*. Philadelphia: J. B. Lippincott Co., 1917.

South Carolina and the Sea: Day by Day Toward Five Centuries, 1492–1985 A.D. Edited by J. Percival Petit. Isle of Palms, SC: Le Petit Maison Publishers, Ltd., 1986.

The South Carolina Encyclopedia. A Project of the Humanities Council SC. Edited by Walter Edgar. Columbia: University of South Carolina Press, 2006.

Verner, Elizabeth O'Neill. *Prints and Impressions of Charleston*. Columbia, SC: Bostick and Thornley, 1945.

Woodard, Colin. *The Republic of Pirates: Being the True and Surprising Story of the Caribbean Pirates and the Man Who Brought Them Down*. Orlando, FL: Houghton Mifflin Harcourt Publishing Company, 2007.

Wright, Louis B. *The Cultural Life of the American Colonies*. Mineola, NY: Dover Publications, Inc., 2002.

Zepke, Terrance. *Pirate of the Carolinas: Second Edition*. Sarasota, FL: Pineapple Press, Inc., 2005.

Print Publications

Arnold, Sara. "A Brief History of the Carolina Art Association and the Gibbes Museum of Art in Charleston, SC." *Carolina Arts*, September 2005.

Behre, Robert. "Retracing the Charleston Steps of the Last Surviving General from the American Revolution." *Post and Courier*, October 30, 2018, Updated September 14, 2020.

Curtis, Julia. "A Note on Henry Holt." *South Carolina Historical Magazine* 79, no. 1 (1978): 1–5. www.jstor.org/stable/27567474.

Eastman, Peg. "Historic Shepheard's Tavern a Key Broad Street Site." *Charleston Mercury*, June 12, 2019.

Ferrari, Mary C. "Charity, Folly, and Politics: Charles Town's Social Clubs on the Eve of the Revolution." *South Carolina Historical Magazine* 112, no. 1/2 (2011): 50–83. www.jstor.org/stable/23057400.

"Footlight Players Present 16th Season." *The Charlestonian*, Charleston Chamber of Commerce, November 1947.

Greene, Harlan. "A Musical Genius, Remembered." *Charleston Magazine*, May 2016.

"Landmark of Exposition Being Razed for Bricks." *News and Courier*, October 27, 1929.

Miles, Suzannah Smith. "Off to the Races." *Charleston Living Magazine*, Jan-Feb 2021.

Mouzon, Harold A. "The Carolina Art Association: Its First Hundred Years." *South Carolina Historical Magazine* 59, no. 3 (1958): 125–38. www.jstor.org/stable/27566176.

Seekings, Michele. "Behind the Wall: Discovered Murals Brought Back to Life." *Art Mag*, March 11, 2020.

Shields, David. "Charleston's First Top Chefs." *Charleston Magazine*, December 2013.

Stockton, Robert P. "The Anson of Ansonborough, The Lord of the Suburb." *Preservation Progress* 55, no. 3, Preservation Society of Charleston, September 2010.

"Trip Up the Ashley River." *Charleston Courier*, April 25, 1872.

Online Publications

"Alexander Garden." History of Early American Landscape Design. National Gallery of Art. Accessed June 10, 2021. https://heald.nga.gov/mediawiki/index .php/Alexander_Garden.

Berg, Dave. "Lt. W.T. Sherman and Charleston." Charleston Military History Highlight. Association of the United States Army, Coastal South Carolina Chapter, December 13, 2018. https://www.ausa.org/charleston-sc-chapter /blog/charleston-military-history-highlight-lt-w-t-sherman-and-charleston.

Butler, Nic, PhD. "Captain Thomas Hayward's Poetic Description of 1769 Charles Town." Charleston County Public Library: Charleston Time Machine, April 16, 2021.https://www.ccpl.org/charleston-time-machine/captain-thomas-hayward -s-poetic-description-1769-charles-town.

———. "The Carolina Coffee House of London." Charleston County Public Library: Charleston Time Machine, January 31, 2020. https://www.ccpl.org /charleston-time-machine/carolina-coffee-house-london.

———. "Charleston's First Ice Age." Charleston County Public Library: Charleston Time Machine, January 19, 2018. https://www.ccpl.org/charleston -time-machine/charlestons-first-ice-age.

———. "George Washington in Charleston, 1791." Charleston County Public Library: Charleston Time Machine, February 9, 2018. https://www.ccpl.org /charleston-time-machine/george-washington-charleston-1791

———. "James Hoban's Charleston Home." Charleston County Public Library: Charleston Time Machine, March 16, 2018. https://www.ccpl.org /charleston-time-machine/james-hobans-charleston-home

———. "Street Cars and Trolleys on Sullivan's Island, 1875–1927." Charleston County Public Library: Charleston Time Machine, April 19, 2019. https://www.ccpl.org/charleston-time-machine/street-cars-and-trolleys -sullivans-island-1875-1927#_edn1.

———. "Tracing the Roots of the 'Charleston' Dance." Charleston County Public Library: Charleston Time Machine, July 17, 2020. https://www.ccpl.org /charleston-time-machine/tracing-roots-charleston-dance

Citations for "Holt" in "The Performing Arts in Colonial American Newspapers, 1690–1783." *South Carolina Gazette*, dates: November 9, 1734; November 15, 1735; March 27, 1735; April 3, 1736; November 27, 1736; December

4, 1736; February 2, 1737; April 23, 1737; April 30, 1737; May 21, 1737. https://www.cdss.org/elibrary/PacanNew/Index/HOLT.htm

"Dubose Heyward House, Charleston County (76 Church St., Charleston)." South Carolina Department of Archives and History: National Register Properties in South Carolina. www.nationalregister.sc.gov/charleston/S10817710041/

"Glimpses of the South Carolina, Interstate and West Indian Exposition." Digital image (pamphlet). Library of Congress, 1902. https://lcdl.library.cofc.edu /lcdl/catalog/lcdl:26290

Jones, Mark R. "Fun Alcohol Facts." Mark Jones Books. Accessed May 22, 2021. https://markjonesbooks.com/fun-alcohol-facts/

——. "Today in Charleston History: January 17." Mark Jones Books. Accessed May 22, 2021. https://markjonesbooks.com/2015/01/17/today-in -history-january-17/.

"McCrady's Tavern and Long Room." South Carolina Historical Properties Record. http://schpr.sc.gov/index.php/Detail/properties/11893.

"Movie Theaters in Charleston, SC." Cinema Treasures. http://cinematreasures.org /theaters/united-states/south-carolina/charleston?status=all.

"The Original She-Crab Soup Recipe." Charming Inns Blog, May 1, 2019. https://www.charminginns.com/blog/she-crab-soup-recipe

"Planter's Punch." *Fun!* magazine, September 1878.

"South Carolina History Timeline." eReference Desk. Accessed June 5, 2021. https://www.ereferencedesk.com/resources/state-history-timeline/south-car olina.html.

Sparks, Randy J. "Gentleman's Sport: Horse Racing in Antebellum Charleston." *South Carolina Historical Magazine* 93, no. 1 (1992): 16. www.jstor.org.proxy .wm.edu/stable/27568264.

Videos

Edison, Thomas A. "Panoramic View of Charleston Exposition." Library of Congress Motion Picture, Broadcasting and Recorded Sound Division. Library of Congress Control Number 00563604. Digital ID: http://hdl.loc.gov/loc .mbrsmi/awal.2132. https://www.loc.gov/item/00563604.

"FDR's Visit to 'Hobcaw' Mr. Bernard Baruch's Barony near Georgetown, SC." Archival footage from the FDR Presidential Library, video 135, 1944, added 3/9/2010. https://archive.org/details/gov.fdr.135.

INDEX

ACKNOWLEDGMENTS

It is with much respect and admiration that I give thanks for the local historians, fellow Charleston history authors (past and present), tour guides, and tourism professionals, whose love of our city shines brightly in all their work.

I am grateful to the Charleston Before 1945 group, whose enduring fascination with All Things Historical Charleston inspired this book. Many a rabbit hole have their posts sent me down, and I am all the richer for it.

ABOUT THE AUTHOR

Shelia Watson is a writer, editor, and screenwriter who is blessed to be a resident of the best city in the world, Charleston, South Carolina. The pleasurable pastime she enjoys most is walking down the streets of Charleston reading every historical plaque on every building. When not visiting the nearby gardens, museums, and waterfront parks, she and her husband enjoy time gardening and spoiling their grandkids.